Barefoot in November

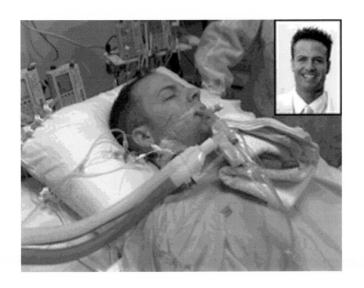

Barefoot in November

A Memoir

Benjamin J. Carey

This is a true story to the best of the author's recollections.

Barefoot in November: A Memoir.

ISBN-13: 978-0-615-45084-1

In Memory of John Ritter,
And Dedicated to my Wife and Children.

PREFACE

Thanks to John Ritter's legacy, there is a movement happening to increase awareness of aortic aneurysms, and improve screening for them. As a result, people like me have avoided dying from the condition. After John died his brother was screened and also found to have an aortic aneurysm which was immediately corrected through elective surgery. Due to increasing evidence that there may be a hereditary component to the condition, it is imperative that family members get screened. In the wake of John's passing, his wife Amy Yasbeck established the *John Ritter Foundation*, and the *John Ritter Research Program; two entities* dedicated to the field of aortic disease.

Many people die from aortic aneurysms because they are unaware that they have it. The cause of death in many of these cases is broadly labeled afterward as a "heart attack" because an x-ray of the heart is needed for an official diagnosis. There are often no symptoms until it is too late. For example, John Ritter was rushed to the hospital with symptoms of a heart attack, and because the doctors treated him for a heart attack instead of an aortic dissection, he died. If John or the doctors were aware of his condition they could have performed surgery to save his life.

A year ago I was diagnosed with an ascending aortic aneurysm. I was thirty-seven years old and in otherwise perfect health. I was lean, athletic, and in better shape than most people half my age. I never would have thought in a million years that I would soon be lying on an operating table cut open like a rack of lamb, with a stranger holding pieces of my beating heart and soul in his hands; while my pregnant wife and two young children pondered the uncertainties of life. This was an event that caused us all to wonder, even if we didn't say it out loud; what life would be like without me. This is the story of the life threatening event, the people and stories in between, and how I went on to run the New York City Marathon on the one year anniversary of my open heart surgery.

ACKNOWLEDGEMENTS

I would like to thank my primary doctor Mark Singer, and my cardiologist Kenneth Walsh who together found and diagnosed my aneurysm. I'm also grateful to Dr. Allan Stewart my surgeon, for allowing me to spend more minutes on earth, and most importantly for encouraging me to "live" after surgery. Thanks to my wife Nicole for dealing with the emotional rollercoaster related to my diagnosis and surgery, and for never leaving my bedside when I needed her. There can also never be enough thanks to my mom, stepdad Ed, and "mom S.", for being there in every way for me. Thanks to my three children, my sister, my brother, my sister-in-law, mother-in-law, and father-in-law. Thanks to my brother-in-law James Rutha for helping to convince me to have the surgery in November when I wanted to wait until January; only to be shocked after pathology tests came back on the aortic tissue that I wouldn't have made it past Thanksgiving. Thanks also to David Butler and Sung Kim for their unconditional support and concern. Thanks to Ken Sawchuck my friend who had the same surgery and gave me advice and emotional support along the way. Thanks to Danielle Macagnone and all of our close friends (I'm afraid if I try to list them all I may forget someone because the list of wonderful people is so long) who brought dinner to our house for ten consecutive nights after I came home from the hospital. Thanks to Erik Pedersen, Greg Sivin, Sal & Ali Merlino, Jen Fornasieri, Dr. Lisa Johnson, and every other person who put their own life on hold to visit me in the hospital. I was surprised, and their visits meant a lot. Thanks to everyone who ever asked how I was doing then, and now. You can never know how much these little gestures of kindness mean until you've had a "life changer" yourself. I wish anyone in this position the blessing of being surrounded by extraordinary people like I was.

Thanks to all of the remarkable people at *New York-Presbyterian* hospital. It's true that "amazing things are happening" there. The doctors, nurses, technicians, receptionists, security guards, and even the man who transported me in the wheelchair all set the bar higher than expected. I felt like a celebrity because of how they treated me. This is a tribute to the leaders there who are building a hospital "culture" that is unprecedented. Being treated like a family member by hospital staff is mind blowing.

Thank you to Margaret Oliva from the American Heart Association. Thanks to Mom and Ed for registering us for the Marathon and getting the ball rolling. Thanks to the people below who donated to the A.H.A. charity and supported us in our New York City Marathon bid, especially Russell and Claudia DiBenedetto who made the first and most significant donation. Aunt Claudia is a cancer survivor and she identified first hand with facing mortality at a young age, and offered kind words of support throughout my ordeal. Also thank you to Jay and Traci Kufeld who donated VIP tickets for finish line seating on race day.

I'd also like to give *a pound* to my editors and the staff at Center Street Publishing. Without them this book would not have been possible. They believed in me and put a smile on my face when I was on two hours sleep and at wits end. There is a rumor about my executive editor being such a perfectionist that she circles errors in library books and returns them, so if you ever come across one you know who did it.

Thank you American Heart Association
NYC Marathon Donors:

Edwin & Laurie Hersh
Russell & Claudia DiBenedetto
Christina Stearns
Denise Smith
Gisele Colarossi
The Delaneys
Bob and Kris Tallman
The Degarays
Tim and Eva Kennedy
Judy Layton
Jay & Traci Kufeld

It's only as bad as you make it.

Barefoot in November

IT WAS ANOTHER DAY OF BUSINESS AS USUAL as I helped get the kids off to school. I was wrapping myself in a towel after my shower and the door slowly opened. My two year old son Preston stood in the half open door rubbing his eyes. "Hi buddy!" I said with the tone of having just won the lottery. He stood there smiling.

"Hi dad! I want breakfast," he said in his little *Elmer Fudd* voice. He is a handsome little boy with chiseled features and spiky blondish hair. He has an all-American look like he had fallen out of a Tommy Hilfiger advertisement. He stood there smiling up at me scratching his bare belly. It was the same routine every morning. He would immediately start rambling when he woke up, like it was two in the afternoon. I would be the first person in the shower, and no matter how quiet I tried to be, he always woke up and met me at the door or in the hallway. The first words out of his mouth were about food. Every day he woke up hungry and in the same unbelievable mood. As soon as his eyes opened he was on overdrive as if each morning was Christmas. I went on to rouse the princess, my five year old daughter Milan. She is very tall for her age, with deep green eyes, and thick sandy-blonde locks down to her butt. She on the other hand is like me. It took me a little bit to get her going in the morning and she could be cranky. I thought it was a fair trade though for the beauty she exuded. Nicole had already left for work, and since I started a little later, I got the kids out the door to school and daycare.

I pulled out of the driveway in pursuit of a coffee, to start another day of chasing the American dream. The only thing different that day was that I had a stress test scheduled for after work. I had been feeling pretty drained, and I attributed it to working hard and being spread so thin. I was involved in three different businesses. I didn't come from money and was fighting tooth and nail to build a life for my family in the affluent north shore of Long Island. I wasn't sickly but apparently my fatigue became noticeable, so my wife harassed me into going for a physical earlier that month. The results of the physical are what led to the appointment for the stress test. My doctor recommended I get a stress test as a precautionary measure to rule out any heart issues that could be associated with the fatigue. There is a history of heart disease in my family, and he said he was just being thorough. I didn't think anything was wrong with me, least of all a heart condition. I was in great shape. I exercised, participated in occasional road races and various sports leagues, and I took care of myself. I thank God that Dr. Mark Singer chose to send me for a stress test after the exam, in spite of having a specimen of physical excellence in front of him. He was the first of a few people, that if it were not for them, I may not be alive today. My wife and I have always sought out progressive, proactive doctors like Dr. Singer, and this was a perfect example why. Doctors like him are passionate about what they do, they practice preventative medicine, they keep abreast of the latest developments and technologies, and they have a compassionate bedside manner. They haven't succumbed to the status quo that in my opinion has become the popular standard of care.

After my coffee stop I worked a half day, and then went to the doctor's office for my stress test. I was annoyed that I had to waste time on the appointment because I didn't feel like I had any health issues or reason to be there. It didn't dawn on me even for a second that the stress test would reveal anything. The last thing I wanted to do was be at the doctor's office after work. Nicole had just begun dissolving a business that didn't work out, and I should have been home helping her deal with it.

I arrived on time for the appointment and was told to have a seat. I sat on a vinyl chair in the waiting room playing with my blackberry, and wondering what the hell I was doing sitting around with a bunch of geriatrics. I didn't have anything against them, but I didn't belong there and was not happy about it. I felt uncomfortable and out of place. I looked at the old man sitting across from me. He had sparse gray hair and was wearing a plaid shirt with a pen protector in the pocket. He wore plastic glasses with thick lenses that sat crooked on his nose as he thumbed through a New Yorker magazine. I smiled at him and thought, *What are you in for buddy? Clogged arteries? Bypass? Pacemaker?* Then I glanced over to an old woman with a cane who was squinting at the television in the room, and she noticed me out of the corner of her eye. I stuck out like a sore thumb. She smiled, and then kept smiling and staring, smiling and staring. She was probably wondering what the hell I was doing there. I caught up on the news while I was sitting there, and then the woman at the desk called my name and she brought me down a long hallway and into the testing lab.

The woman who would be doing my stress test greeted me as I entered the room. She was in her forties and wearing blue scrubs.

"Hi there," she said.

"Hi."

"Have you ever had a stress test before?"

"No," I answered.

"Why are you having one?"

"I had a physical recently and was complaining about fatigue and my doctor suggested it. I think it's silly, but my wife has been on my case and hopefully it will appease her."

"Well, this is quick and easy," she said. "I'm just going to stick some electrodes on your chest, and have you walk on the treadmill."

"No problem." I said.

The woman had a very warm personality. We chatted more about our children and the school district, and then she asked me to take off my shirt and hop up on the examination table. She explained the test in more detail as she hooked me up to a dozen wires and electrodes which were placed on my bare chest. She explained that she would be taking sonogram images of my heart as I walked through progressively harder stages on the treadmill.

The test began, and it was a joke. I walked, and walked unfazed. I made it through all of the stages as the woman and her assistant looked on in amazement. I felt like a big hero until it dawned on me who these women were accustomed to having for patients. I finished the final stage, barely breaking a sweat and then immediately hopped up onto the examination table for the woman to get images of my heart in stress mode. "Wow, amazing!" the woman's assistant said, "No one ever makes it that far into the test."

I smiled like a big idiot. "In college I was an NCAA All-American in Cross Country," I said. The test ended and my heart rate came down. I couldn't wait to be done with all the nonsense.

"Stay here, the doctor just needs to read this and you'll be on your way," said the woman. She left and there was silence, except for the crinkling of the white paper covering the table I sat on. It seemed like she was gone a very long time. It must have been at least fifteen to twenty minutes, toward the end of which I could hear hushed conversations going on outside the door. I was getting annoyed. For a second I thought, *What if?* And then I quickly laughed it off. *No way in hell; no chance.* Then the door opened and the woman walked in with the chief cardiologist, Dr. Walsh. He is an older man with good looks, graying hair, and a nice tan. He is very articulate, and the epitome of what you would expect a cardiologist to be.

"Hi I'm Dr. Walsh," he said as he extended his hand straight out. He was all about business. He went straight to the sonogram machine and looked at the video on the monitor. "Have you ever had a stress test before?" he asked.

"No," I said, "but when I was in college they did do a sonogram on my heart because I was getting headaches. They wanted to rule out heart issues because of my family history of heart disease. The results turned out to be normal, and had nothing to do with the headaches. They went away on their own. The doctor did say though, that I had a slightly enlarged aorta and left ventricle but that it was common in endurance athletes and 3.2cm was within the range of normal."

He turned and looked at me for a moment and said, "No, not this big." His eyes quickly went back to the monitor. "This is not normal," he said.

"What do you mean?" I said, "How big is it?"

"Its 5.2cm at the root, you're going to have to see someone about this."

"We can watch it. It can't be that bad right?" I asked.

"It is above the acceptable range," Dr. Walsh explained. "Normally surgery is recommended for measurements above 5.0cm, however you need to have a CT Scan in order to confirm our findings as it is more accurate than the sonogram."

I stared straight ahead and just about shit my pants! *Oh my God! Impossible! This is nothing to worry about,* I thought.

"What if I leave and never come back or do anything about it?" I asked Dr. Walsh.

"You wouldn't want to do that; you have kids and a family. Here take a look, you see this?" He pointed to the monitor. I was horrified. *How could I deny it? How could I pretend this didn't exist when I was staring right at it?* I looked at the beating heart and the aneurysm was clear as day. It was huge and appeared as big as the ventricle. There it was an indisputable black and white image on the screen. I just stared and watched the heartbeat. Everything was working, but there was no mistaking the huge bulge on the outside of the valve. I was scared. It was so big that it looked like another chamber of the heart, only on the outside. *How were the little flaps of skin that make up the valve working, under such "stretched" conditions I wondered?* Dr. Walsh's voice snapped me out of the trance "You'll have to schedule a CT scan, on your way out."

After he had left, the woman who performed the test turned to me. "I'm sorry," she said. "You have a family to think about, and you really need to see someone." She walked me out, and back down the hallway to the lobby where we said goodbye. I wasn't sure what I was going to do, or if I was even going to tell anyone. My mind was racing. When I got to the car I immediately got on my blackberry and started researching aortic aneurysms to find out more. I had learned early on in life to be diligent and to never accept the status quo.

I drove out of the parking lot, blackberry in hand; yelling at the top of my lungs. "Fuck!" I laughed hysterically out loud, and my eyes welled up with tears. I laughed again, and then got abruptly serious on the blackberry. I drove slowly, weaving all over the road as I scoured Google for information. By the time I arrived home I had seen enough online to know that I was definitely fucked.

I turned into the driveway, and put the truck in park. I was home, and as usual the sight of it had a calming effect on me. Home is a big white Georgian style colonial with huge white pillars on the front porch and a widow's walk overlooking the front yard. There is a hip roof with *dog-houses jutting out, eyebrow windows,* an English inspired chimney, and black shutters on every window. Wrought iron lanterns and four wooden rocking chairs complete it. I had designed and built the place myself, and I just sat there for a moment taking in the rich landscaping, colorful flowers popping, and the smell of the fresh cut lawn. I watched the wicker ceiling fan on the front porch rotating slowly, and I hung my head and sighed. Then I opened the truck door to go inside and see the family.

The kids were sleeping when I got in and my wife Nicole was loading the dishwasher in the kitchen. She looked beautiful as usual, even after a day of running Carey Inc. She is one-hundred percent Italian with long brown hair and briar colored eyes the shape of *Jennifer Aniston's.* She is of average height with an athletic figure, and a raspy voice which I adore. She has fire in her personality and a way about her that you would want her on your team at any cost. We are best friends. When she saw me she immediately asked, "So, how was it?"

"It was okay. They said I was one of the only patients to complete all stages of the graded stress test," I laughed.

"Good," she said, "so then everything is okay."

I laughed and looked down for a second. I didn't want to get into it with her because I knew it would create a whole production. We dealt with stress in very different and unique ways. I could cope with bombs going off next to me and still find a way to stay focused, whereas she processed things differently.

"Everything is okay?" she asked again. I realized I wasn't getting out of this one. I sighed and looked her dead in the eye. I paused. Tears welled up in my eyes.

"Not really."

"What do you mean?" she asked.

I shook my head.

"Ben what is going on?"

"My aorta is enlarged, but I don't think it's that bad. They want me to have a CT scan."

Tears rolled down Nicole's eyes and she had to lean on the counter between us to hold herself up. She came around to my side and hugged me.

"Whatever," I said angrily. I wasn't in the mood for affection or sympathy. "It's going to be okay. I'm not worried, and you shouldn't be. Its only one opinion and I'm diesel. I can run circles around people. Look at me!"

"When do you have to go for the CT scan?" asked Nicole.

"I don't know I have to make an appointment. Maybe the CT scan will show a smaller measurement since it's more accurate." I stood there for what felt like an eternity, as she sobbed and the world caved in around me. *Was this it? Was my life over? Is this the so called moment that we all arrive at some day in our lives? Was it my time? After making it this far in life was it the end of the road for me? How the hell could this be happening?* It was like a bad dream.

That night I lay awake in bed for hours after everyone had gone to sleep. It was warm for April. The windows were open and I watched the breeze play with the long curtains on the windows, tousling them back and forth. The moonlight shone through the *dog-house* window onto the vaulted ceiling, casting shadows off the slowly turning ceiling fan. It was peaceful, and I asked God for help.

The day of the CT scan was another miserable day. Nicole insisted on coming with me and we argued because I told her I wanted to go alone. I really wanted her there for me, but I didn't want her to be upset with the results. I could deal with anything, but I was worried about her. Deep down I knew it was going to be bad. We had the test done locally at an x-ray clinic that we were referred to. When we arrived Nicole was overbearing and took control of checking me in. We bickered about it in the waiting room. It made her feel better being in control of something that soon neither of us would be able to manage. After a short wait I went in for the scan. I was frightened. I hated visits to the doctor and hospital, especially when I was the patient. I was handed a gown to wear and shown a machine that I would lay down on and be passed through on a platter like a rotisserie chicken.

"We will be inserting an I.V. in your arm, and during the process you will be injected with dye for the imaging. You may feel an urge to urinate, but that's normal," said the male technician. He was dressed business casual, and was not very friendly. I felt more like a customer at the place, not a patient.

I started laughing, "Oh that's great," I said. "I haven't felt that way since I woke up this morning." The drone laughed with me. In the end the experience was unpleasant but not horrendous. The horrendous part was not the CT scan, but the idea of being there for a life threatening reason. They didn't give CT scans for the common cold.

Later that day Dr. Walsh called and informed us that the aneurysm was not 5.2cm, but was 5.5cm according to the CT scan. Nicole took the call, and before she even hung up I was laughing hysterically! "Holy shit!" I said to her. "Can you believe this shit?" I continued laughing, and tears rolled down her cheeks.

"You're an asshole, this is not funny," she said.

"Whatever, I'm not worried about it. I've conquered worse problems."

"You need to see a surgeon Ben."

"No I don't. I'm not doing shit until I do some research. I'm not going to go under the knife based on one opinion without doing my own research on this. Nobody is cutting me open yet. I'm a big guy and scientifically speaking these readings can't be the same for people of all different sizes. That wouldn't make sense. I'm an athlete; of course my aorta is going to be bigger. With all of the training and abuse I put my body through in the past it's to be expected."

She looked me in the eye and said "We need to deal with this together, don't be selfish; you have us to think about, not just yourself," and she walked out of the room.

Over the next few weeks I spent countless nights on the computer until the wee hours of the morning searching for answers. I was looking for someone to tell me it was okay; someone to tell me I didn't have to be cut open. That person was *Dr. X*. I had found him online and even watched him perform open heart surgery on one of his website videos. He was a pioneer and expert in *The Ross Procedure*, a special technique where they cut off your pulmonary valve and re-attach it at the site of your defective aortic valve. The thinking behind this is that your congenital valve lasts longer and doesn't break down like animal valves. I sought out *Dr. X* because he seemed progressive, thorough, and cutting edge. He was a very respected and popular surgeon. I emailed him and he responded promptly and invited me in for a consult. I was adamant about not having to have this surgery, and in search of any evidence or person who would support my mission of denial. In the weeks leading up to my appointment with *Dr. X*, I had done a wealth of research on my condition. I had read the stories of John Ritter, Ronnie Turiaf, and others who had aortic aneurysms. Some lived, some died. I also watched numerous videos, visited heart forums, and uncovered a bunch of medical journal articles. One article in particular from a medical journal was exactly what I was looking for. I clung to it like a security blanket. It was a study on how novel measurement of aortic aneurysm size relative to size and weight predicted the potential for rupture. In layman terms it was a study that I interpreted to say that your aortic root size was relative to your body size and weight.

Nicole and I arrived at *Dr. X*'s office in Manhattan and his secretary greeted us. His office was located in a special wing of the hospital. We filled out forms in a huge ornate room with cathedral ceilings and plush chairs. *Probably paid for from all the heart surgeries,* I thought resentfully. *I wasn't going to be paying for anyone's ass to sit there.* I had gotten bitter about my predicament and my attitude reflected it. Before I knew it *Dr. X* had arrived and the three of us exchanged smiles and handshakes. He is tall, salt and pepper hair, with a square jaw and thick rimless glasses that were polished to perfection. He doesn't have an accent, but something about him reminds me of the south. He seems like a cowboy in a $2,000 suit, and his manner was cool and laid back, just the way it was during the surgeries I watched him perform in the online videos. He took us to an examination room, listened to my heart, and gave me a basic checkup. Then we joined him in his office for the consultation.

Nicole and I locked eyes on him waiting for him to speak as he shuffled papers and prepared his computer. "Well you definitely have an aneurysm at the root of your aorta. The question is whether or not you need surgical intervention," he said. I interrupted, and went off reciting all of the research I had done, and how I didn't want to be cut open unless I was about to die, etc.

"Doc, I don't want to offend you but I'm not like other people who would jump off a bridge if their doctor told them to," I said. "Performing heart surgery to you guys is like changing your underwear, and I don't want to have this done unless you tell me right now that if I walk out of here I'm going to drop dead." Nicole sat next to me with a look of embarrassment. I didn't give a fuck. It wasn't that I was being disrespectful, but with my life at risk, all bets were off. I didn't care if I sounded like an asshole or not. My life was at stake.

He smiled and looked at me. "I understand," he said. "If you feel that way, based on what I see we can just watch it, do another CT scan in six months, and see if it grows." He proceeded to explain a number of reasons why he felt that it was okay to delay surgery. He brought up the CT scan on his monitor and showed me how the image of the aorta was taken on a slight angle and how that could have given a slightly inflated reading.

"Anytime you take a measurement of a tube on an angle you get a bigger diameter," he said. "Also, since this is a still image, there's no telling if your heart was in systolic or diastolic mode which could also affect the measurement."

Brilliant! I thought. Then he referred to the study from the medical journal that I had emailed him on the size of the aorta vs. body size. He had printed it out, and showed me where I measured on the chart, taking into consideration the size of my body and aorta.

"You are not even in the one percent risk category, and even if it grew, you wouldn't be in the highest risk category based on the chart," he said.

"Great news!" I said. I looked at Nicole and I could tell she was annoyed that I characteristically dominated and influenced the meeting. She felt that I was holding on to anything in order to avoid the knife, and it was keeping my whole family on edge.

"It's okay Nicole, I'll get another CT scan in six months. It's going to be okay," I said.

Nicole asked *Dr. X* more questions, as I zoned out wondering how much a heart surgeon makes, what this guy's life was like, and how it felt to play God. He was one of the most sought after surgeons in the country, and it was an honor to sit with him. We made a little more small talk about our families, and then thanked him for his time and left.

"Isn't that great?" I said to Nicole as we were walking out of the building.

"Great? You're kidding right? You are definitely going to get another opinion right?"

"Why?" I said. "I'm comfortable with his diagnosis. What's the point?"

"You should get another opinion Ben, you're in denial. This isn't you. If this were anything else in your life you would not stop at one opinion. It's not in your nature, why start now? When you built our house you got three different prices on a 2x4 from three different suppliers; I mean seriously."

"I'm fine now," I said. "You heard him, you saw the research. I'm not being ridiculous. I'll go in six months and get another CT scan."

I woke up the next morning determined to get back to normal, and for quite a while it was business as usual. Except that is, for everyone in my family coaxing me to get more medical attention for the condition. My mom was the worst at getting on my case. She had been through five open heart surgeries with my brother, knew about the highly publicized case of John Ritter, and felt that I was a ticking time bomb. She called me every couple of days to harass me, and when she wasn't calling me, she was pleading with my wife to get me to a surgeon.

I continued to work like a dog. I had just opened a gym franchise with some partners, and they made me the Chief Marketing Officer. I was also working on some internet projects, and wholesaling designer eyewear. The freedom of being an independent contractor in the eyewear business allowed me to arrange my schedule to manage everything, and I loved the fact that I didn't have to answer to any micromanagers. Previously I had worked in the Sports Club business in Manhattan during an initial public offering and it was a toxic environment. It was like a war and a soap opera between all the micromanagers. They were control freaks who made their way by following plans well, not by being the most talented or intelligent in the company.

In the eyewear business there were rumors that my boss felt threatened by my upward mobility in the company, and I knew when I told him about my heart condition and potential absence that he would see it as an opportunity to execute me. I had great relationships with my clients, was a top producer, and I was a family man; something the principals of the company admired. He had a failed marriage and made no secret of dating the secretary at the home office, and it deepened the contrast between us. A few weeks had passed since my diagnosis, and one day I met him for lunch. I told him what was going on with me, and all he could say was "I have a buddy who I play hockey with who had a condition like that, would you like me to have him call you?"

"Sure, it would be great to speak with someone who had to deal with the same thing," I said. Time passed, and I never heard from his buddy, and he never brought up my condition again, not even to ask how my family or I was doing.

My condition remained the same, without any notable symptoms of the aneurysm. I continued with an on and off again exercise program, but I had become nervous when lifting weights. In the back of my head I knew there was a possibility of blowing up the aneurysm and bleeding to death from my heart pumping blood into my chest cavity, but I didn't know how to live otherwise. The way I saw it God had a plan for me and it was already written whether I would meet my demise or get more good years with my family. I didn't let fear threaten my ability to stay in shape. I wasn't being careless, I had just surrendered to the fact that things would either work out, or my life was meant to end like a Shakespearean tragedy. *Dr. X* didn't forbid me from lifting weights, he just said be smart; don't lift hundreds of pounds.

In July the eyewear company made cutbacks across the country, and my boss made sure I was one of them in spite of my performance. It was horrible timing because Nicole had closed her business and was not working, and I had been diagnosed with the aneurysm only a few weeks prior. The guy didn't even have the decency to give me the news himself; he had his boss do it. The incident consumed me, overshadowing my ability to deal with anything else including my diagnosis. I couldn't understand how someone could be so heartless under the circumstances and I was determined to right this wrong. I wasn't looking for pity from anyone, just a little understanding. I immediately filed a lawsuit against the company, which was resolved to my satisfaction a few months later.

I spent most of my time after that with my partners in the health club venture, Greg and Alex. We were already looking at opening a second location in a neighboring town, and if I stayed with them they were offering me a percentage of each new club we opened. They were good guys, and we had a lot in common. We all came from poor backgrounds and shared a strong work ethic and entrepreneurial spirit. Before embarking on the gym venture Greg was a successful Wall Street analyst and Alex was an acupuncturist. They were one-hundred percent Russian. On one notable night out with our wives we went to an authentic Russian club called Tatiana's in Brooklyn. It was located on the ocean in Brighton Beach and was something out of a movie. The place reeked of money as Bentleys, and Rolls Royces dropped patrons at the curb. Upon our arrival Greg and Alex shook hands with the man at the door, exchanged greetings in Russian, and we were escorted down a private entrance. Inside, fish swam under the glass floor and there wasn't a bad looking person in the place. For the next three hours Russian food flowed non-stop from the kitchen. Everything that came out looked like a piece of art; so pretty you didn't want to eat it. We sank our teeth into some of the richest and heaviest dishes ever to hit our palates. A Russian style cabaret show followed, with skimpily clad exotic dancers, fire stunts, and a laser light show. We concluded the evening dancing until the wee hours of the morning and it was a night to remember.

At the end of July my brother-in-law called me to join him in his own new venture, an online advertising agency specializing in schools and finance. I had been waiting to be tapped by him for a long time, and I was ecstatic about it. It was only a few years back that he had been living in his grandmother's basement, and in a very short time he bought a two million dollar Manhattan condo, a BMW, and a couple of watches that would equal a small down payment on a house. I respected him and what he had done. He was a closer, not an order taker who rode on the coat tails of others. He was liquid, and unlike most of the people with money I had met in Long Island, he made it himself. He wasn't a spoiled brat who grew up with BMW's, summer camps, and nannies. Nothing was handed to him by mommy and daddy nor was it inherited, and I loved that about him.

A few nights a week I worked late in the Hoboken office so I stayed overnight at my place in Manhattan. We adored the city, so we kept an apartment there after we had moved across the bridge to Long Island. Nicole wasn't thrilled about the routine, but she knew the potential. Her brother had built a nice life relatively quickly, and had now brought me into his circle. Internet advertising was laden with twenty and *thirty-somethings* driving Ferraris, owning vacation homes, and loving their work. You didn't need an Ivy League degree, just a strong work ethic, ability to sell, and be with a young company. It was a great opportunity to get into a business I knew I could be influential in. James and his partners were established veterans, but more than that they were incredible human beings. It was a great environment to be in. As far as my aneurysm was concerned, I really didn't know what to do about it. I was beginning to feel symptoms, but they weren't debilitating. The situation was such a contradiction. If I was in poor health or had dire symptoms I would have succumbed to having the operation, but I was so young and healthy.

Summer finally came to an end, and fall began its descent. One evening after a late night in the office, I decided to stay at my place in the city, and on the way to the apartment I stopped at Barnes and Noble near Lincoln Center. I loved this bookstore because it was huge, and it was in my favorite part of the city; the upper west side around Central Park West and Broadway. My apartment was a little farther up, but I spent most of my time in this neighborhood over the past ten years. Once inside, I wandered up and down the escalators to different floors, browsing aimlessly at all of the interesting books. People with the same idea stood in the aisles thumbing through a broad range of topics. Some sat in the aisle cross legged, and others whispered to each other; perhaps talking about politics, art, or quantum physics. Naturally, I found a book to do more research on my condition. I picked up "The Surgeons: Life and Death in a Top Heart Center", by Charles Morris, and headed down to the checkout. While in line waiting to pay, "American Gods" by Neil Gaiman caught my eye, and I threw that up on the counter too. My stomach grumbled and as I left the store I figured I would stop off at the Indian restaurant near my apartment, a favorite ritual on my overnights in the city.

I walked along Central Park West. Fall seemed to arrive early, as if reminding me of my ailing heart condition. The city was beautiful this time of year. As I walked, fallen leaves crunched under my feet, and I could see my breath. I sat down on a bench near the park and took it all in. It was one of those melodramatic moments where I saw my whole life before me. Joggers ran by along the wavy cobblestone walkway, and a man played a saxophone on the corner. Then there was silence. I put my head back and watched the white steam rise from my mouth as I sighed. Tears ran down my cheeks as I watched random leaves fall in slow motion, backlit by the streetlamps. Images of my five year old daughter, and my two year old son swirled in the sky before me. Nicole appeared, and they were all talking to each other in muffled tones. No one acknowledged me. It was a vision of life without me there. I shook my head. *This is unreal,* I thought. *What if I die? Is this it for me? This can't be happening.* I felt like *Jimmy Stewart* in *It's a Wonderful Life,* except that there was no turning off the television when the movie was over. As much as I tried; I knew that the chance of escaping this assault on my life was not likely. I stood up, shaking it off, and continued on to the Indian Restaurant.

When I arrived, the familiar Indian man greeted me at the door smiling, and motioned to my table as if waiting for me since I left two weeks ago. He is a kind man with burnished brown skin, and deep lines. He had a long beard and dark mysterious eyes with no whites or color as if a character from a *Harry Potter* movie. Dinner there was one of the most relaxing parts of my stressful week. The restaurant was dark, reeked of curry, and was adorned with pounds of heavy velvet and silk. Middle Eastern music twanged as the turbaned staff shuffled along the floor attending to their responsibilities. Connoisseurs of ethnic food know that these small hole-in-the wall places often have better service and more authentic food than the bigger fancier places. At that late hour the restaurant was nearly empty. I sat alone at a candle lit table facing the floor-to-ceiling windows overlooking the street and was waited on like a king. I pulled out *American Gods,* and started reading as the mint drizzled samosas melted in my mouth. I had forced myself into reading more fiction, and books that I normally wouldn't pick out because I felt it made oneself better read.

Coincidentally, it ended up being a bizarre, dark book, which fit in perfectly with what I was going through. I usually ate so much at the restaurant that I could barely breathe. I felt like I needed a C-section, not heart surgery. I was convinced that all of the pressure put extra stress on the aneurysm, but I couldn't help myself. Afterward, I went back to the apartment and just sat there, stuffed. I felt pain in my sternum, and was nervous that I might keel over and be found dead from a gluttonous helping of chicken tikka masala. Still, who could resist. That night I put down *"American Gods"* and picked up *"The Surgeons."* I stayed up until 5:00 a.m. and read the entire book. Besides being informative, it was entertaining and it changed my entire view on life, my condition, and even my brother's past open heart surgeries. *The Surgeons,* by Charles Morris gives a birds-eye view into the world of *New York-Presbyterian's Heart Center.* The author is allowed to perpetrate the cardiac surgery department at the prestigious hospital and chronicle his experience. The book examines the ups and downs of the patients and their families, and the complexities of the surgeries. It also gives the reader an idea of the long hours and grueling demands put on the surgeons. It is a tale of miracles and heartbreaks. In the book Dr. Allan Stewart was painted as a young star who was driven and talented enough to become Chairman of the prestigious department. He had just been promoted to head the aortic surgery program at the hospital. I concluded after reading this book that I needed to see him.

In October I was forced with having to deal with the aneurysm. Up until that point I had forgotten about it, but October was the six month mark. That was when I was supposed to have the second CT scan. My mom, wife, and family were harassing me diligently about getting the second CT scan and another opinion. Unbeknownst to them I had been experiencing bouts of being winded and short of breath. I was also getting dull chest pains behind my sternum with some frequency. I was doing a two hour commute to the office and it was a nightmare. I had to pick from a handful of trains each way, and if I missed one it threw off my schedule by as much as a couple of hours. I was always running to and from the train to avoid missing it. You only know what it is like to spend two whole hours in transit door-to-door if you've done it. You don't see your children in the morning before you leave or in the evening before they go to bed, and as fall sets in it's dark when you leave and when you come home. There's no time for coaching your kids sports team or attending any of the other important things in their lives because you're on the train when they go down. It wasn't pleasant, but business was explosive at the company and I had brought in one of the biggest deals to date. I didn't know it at the time, but lucky for me this deal and the generosity of the company would support me during my medical leave of absence.

It is said that there are often no symptoms of an aortic aneurysm, but contrary to my denial I started having some. If I hadn't been officially diagnosed perhaps I would have mistaken them for something else. I was frightened, but I kept it to myself so as to not worry anyone. I knew I had no choice but to get the second opinion and another CT scan. I resumed my research like a madman on a mission, and I investigated the best hospitals, and the best surgeons. I also looked very closely at the best procedures for my condition. My aorta was tricuspid and had no regurgitation. In essence, the only messed up part of my heart was the huge bulge in the aorta at the root. That was good news, but it was also the most difficult aspect for me to accept since everything else was perfect. No high cholesterol, clogged arteries, nothing; just a freak bulge in the aorta. Based on the fact that my valve was good, I immediately eliminated the *Ross Procedure* or any procedure that included targeting my valve. *If it is not broke, don't fix it* was my mentality. With the physical symptoms slowly setting in, it dawned on me seriously for the first time, that I would not be escaping the knife. I made phone calls, researched online forums, investigated the best techniques, and spent countless sleepless nights at the computer tweaking out until sunrise. Finally I narrowed it down to two doctors that I wanted to see; Dr. Allan Stewart at *New York-Presbyterian* hospital in Manhattan, and Dr. Craig Miller out of *Stanford* hospital in California. They are both experts in all sorts of aortic specific surgeries, and the most sought after aortic surgeons in the country.

Around this time, *Dr. X* called me to schedule the follow-up CT scan, but I cancelled because I had set up an appointment with Dr. Allan Stewart. As nice, and as qualified as *Dr. X* was, I didn't want to have the *Ross Procedure* done, and even if he had considered an alternative I wanted to weigh my options. The more research I did the more good things I learned about Allan Stewart and the *New York-Presbyterian* team and I wanted to see him. Dr. Stewart specialized in a *valve-sparing* procedure for patients like me wherein he would cut out and remove the ballooned aorta and any suspect portions around it, replace it with Dacron tubing, and leave the aortic valve untouched or "spared." I'm not a surgeon, but everything I heard and read about his procedure seemed superior. The Dacron tube that he replaced the aorta with was slid down over the spared valve so as to prevent future degradation or stretching of it. To give you a crude example of this, think of a rubber washer pushed up inside of a toilet paper tube where the tube gives added support on the outside of the washer, preventing it from stretching out. This was an improvement on earlier versions of the procedure where the Dacron tube was simply sewed to the top of the valve and over time it could become stretched out. All of my research led me to believe that Dr. Stewart had the best method of correcting my condition. Dr. Craig Miller was the other renowned doctor I was considering seeing, but I decided not to because he was so far away and because I had read about the large volume of surgeries he performed utilizing artificial valves.

I knew it was important to pick a good surgeon because their techniques differed and variations of the same procedure were common. Experts in the field said that the process bordered on being "an Art." I made an appointment to see Dr. Stewart. I still had hope that I could somehow avoid surgery, so I didn't ask Nicole to accompany me on the appointment. I didn't want her saying "I told you so" if he started on me about needing to have the surgery done. On the other hand though I was slowly coming to grips with the reality that without surgery I might end up like John Ritter.

I left work early one afternoon and made a trip uptown to meet with Dr. Stewart. As I came up out of the subway with the crowd of people, I felt alone. *New York-Presbyterian* occupies a few city blocks, and it took me a moment to find the Millstein Building where I needed to go. The building is an enormous skyscraper with a wraparound driveway in front where people were picking up and dropping off. The size of the building, I thought, seemed symbolic of the magnitude of the surgeries performed inside. I mean how would I have felt if I arrived at a one story flat? I didn't pay too much attention to my surroundings because I was so anxious. Before I knew it I was standing in Dr. Stewart's office being introduced to him. "Is your wife with you?" he asked with a puzzled look on his face.

"No she's not," I answered. "I wanted to speak with you first by myself."

"Okay," he said, still with a somewhat confused look, but seeming like he was catching on to me.

"How bad is my situation?" I asked. "Can I get away with not having surgery?"

I sat down and like two men looking under the hood of a broken hot rod we began a serious conversation about the plumbing in my heart, how bad the problem was, and what my options were. I liked Dr. Stewart immediately. His candor and confidence were complemented by a sympathetic quality that most surgeons don't possess. He didn't have that *I make a thousand dollars an hour so make it quick* attitude. If he were a rock star he would be the type getting yelled at by his manager for taking too much time signing autographs and mingling with fans. We put all of the information on the table, looked at the previous CT scan together, and discussed everything that I had spoken about previously with *Dr. X.* "Listen, the reality is that you need to take care of this," he said. "I can't tell you that it's going to be okay. You really should have surgery now to correct this. We typically perform surgery for aneurysms over 5cm, and yours was 5.5cm six months ago. It's best to have the surgery now while your valve is still intact, before it gets stretched out and you need to have the valve replaced too. That's outside of the fact that you're walking around like a ticking time bomb."

I was shaking inside. Like an idiot I asked "Well what are my options?" as if I didn't hear what the man just said. I didn't ask on purpose, I just didn't know what else to say and it just came out. "Can we do another CT scan and double check everything? Can we at least put this off until January?" I asked. "I have some things going on in the office and I can't afford to be out right now. January would be much better."

"Go home. Think about everything. Talk with your wife, and then come back and have a CT scan here under my supervision. We'll look at the results and if it hasn't grown then we can all talk about it and come up with a plan."

"So I don't need to have the surgery now?" I asked relentlessly. We both stood up because it was nearing the end of our appointment.

"Benjamin, no one is mandating you to have the surgery. Only you can decide that. This condition is not going away though, and you are going to need surgery if you want to avoid a catastrophe. Like I said, talk about this with your wife. I'll give you my cell phone number in case you guys have any questions and if you want to come back in for another CT scan and meeting I'd be glad to meet with you both. If the aneurysm has not grown we can come up with a timeline and a plan for surgery."

With that we shook hands, and I left. It was a long trip home, as I tried to play out over and over in my mind how this whole thing would pan out. *Maybe I would just die and not have to make any decisions or deal with anything,* I thought. For the first time I was no longer sure how this was going to end up. For the past six months I was convinced that I was not going to have to have open heart surgery. Now there were many question marks, and I was driving myself crazy trying to come up with a hypothetical ending. I had no idea where this path was leading, and I didn't have the capacity to deal with it.

Everyone who faces their mortality talks of the change of perspective that happens as a result. After my appointment with Dr. Stewart everything in my life was thrust into the spotlight. Life paused, as if all the different scenes in a movie had been stopped, and I had a chance to evaluate them one by one. I saw that I had achieved what I wanted most in life; a healthy, close-knit family. My wife and children made my world and I lived for them more than anything else. I realized however, that there were some other things that I wanted to address just in case my luck turned bad. I'm not talking about clichés like going skydiving, or climbing the Rockies; I'm talking about relationships and loose ends that needed attention but never got it because of the hustle and bustle of daily life. I made amends where they were due, and put down any long held baggage I had accrued. I also made sure that everyone in my life knew how I felt about them. I seized any opportunity that I could to tell people I loved and appreciated them. I also noted people who failed when put to the test, and if I survived I didn't want to continue wasting time on the superficial relationships. Jason for example was my best friend and best man in my wedding, but he was constantly disappointing me. I knew I would end up drawing lines and moving on. I'm a firm believer in quality over quantity when it comes to friendships. I expect my friends to be the kind of friend I am, and unfortunately or fortunately, depending how you look at it; that weeds out a lot of people. Before my diagnosis, life seemed like an eternity where there would be time for everything, but now with a question mark thrown into the formula, I felt compelled to expedite everything. I hadn't been diagnosed with pancreatic cancer, but aortic open heart surgery was life threatening enough. One of the toughest things I did was reaching out to my father who I hadn't spoken with in over twenty years. I had amassed brutal resentment toward him because of my childhood and a bitter divorce that I had to live through at eleven years old. It's what drove me to be the consummate father, husband, and family man. He had moved from New York to Florida long before we stopped talking. Over the years I had done some investigating and found his address and telephone number. Something compelled me to reach out to him and finish a chapter of my life that was cut short. I wanted to know more about the man who brought me into the world and in the process hopefully learn more about myself. I felt it was time to let bygones be bygones and see if we could move forward. I didn't want to be imprisoned by the negative feelings anymore, and I also didn't want to deprive myself of learning more about my past. The day after my appointment with Dr. Stewart, I called and left a message.

"I'm pretty sure this is the right number to the Careys; this message is for Conrad. Nancy if you should get the message

I would appreciate it if you would pass it on to him. Dad, it's your son Ben calling. It's been a long time, and I wanted to reach out and see if we can start from here to get to know each other again. I know I've left angry messages over the years, but this time I'm not calling to make you pay for everything that happened in my childhood. Give me a call back."

The next day his wife Nancy called me and told me she would pass on the message. I told her my intentions, and also let her know what was going on with my heart. She was sorry to hear that and told me that my dad had his own battles with cancer last year. When we finished our call all I could think about was the amount of time that had passed from the last time I saw my dad. That night I was at the gym working late on marketing initiatives and my cell phone rang. I saw a Florida area code and I knew it was him. I got up from the desk and walked to the front door to go outside and talk. The breakaway glass doors slid open, and I stepped outside into the parking lot, and into another chapter of my life.

"Hello," I said. It was dark and there was a slight breeze. Noise from the coming and going of cars each way on the busy road filled the background. I paced back and forth as I spoke. "Yeah....I just figured enough is enough, and I wanted to see if we could find a way to get to know each other before one of us drops dead."

"Well, I never stopped thinking about you all of these years," said my dad. "I know I was a bad father, but there's nothing I can do about it now, and I don't want to be reminded of it anymore." It was nice to finally here him admit that. I had never heard him say it out loud before. I don't think he was capable of a formal apology. I continued pacing back and forth in front of the building as I spoke.

"You're right," I said. "Things were real bad when I was little, and I haven't forgotten about any of it. That's not the point though. Like I said I just want to see if there's anything left for us in the years we have left. I'd like to see if we can try and have something that resembles a relationship."

"Well, it's nice to hear from you," he said. "Nancy mentioned something about your heart. What is that all about?"

"I have an aortic aneurysm, and it's likely that I'm going to have to have open heart surgery to have it fixed. I still can't believe it, but what can you do? We all know we're going to get 'something' as we age, we just don't know what. It's a crapshoot this game of life."

He asked me details about the condition and the surgery which was typical of my dad. He's a mechanical genius and I knew he needed to ask these questions to understand exactly what was going on. When we finished talking about my heart I could tell he was anxious and felt bad about it. We finished with some small talk about my brother and sister and agreed to keep in touch. I hung up my cell phone and stood outside the gym for a moment and just stared off at the cars passing on the busy road. I ran my fingers through my hair and sighed. I knew it was important for me to contact my dad and address the unfinished chapter in my life, but in the past I was never able to muster up forgiveness or let go of the resentment. After the call I felt a huge weight lifted off me, and bitterness was replaced with optimism.

A week or so had passed, and in that time Nicole had spoken with Dr. Stewart about our meeting. Whatever he said to Nicole had given her a heightened sense of urgency in regard to my condition. Later I would find out that he told her that if he had met with me six months ago he would have suggested immediate surgery because of the size of my aneurysm. Her tone with me switched to a serious one, intolerant of my excuses. She knew that she had an edge now to convince me to get the surgery because I finally found a doctor and procedure that I was comfortable with. She leveraged that and made the appointment for me to have the follow up CT scan and for us to meet with Dr. Stewart together this time.

I took a day off from the office and we left Long Island and drove to *New York-Presbyterian* to meet Dr. Stewart and have the second CT scan. I kept a business as usual attitude with Nicole and acted as if this were just another routine test even though I knew that it was not going to be good. I didn't want to upset her any more than necessary. We chatted about the baby and kids on the drive in, and made small talk. "Hey," I said, "I've been thinking; you know those two accent rocks we put in front of the house for landscaping?"

"Yes?" said Nicole, with a notable anxiety in her voice.

"Well, I think I want to get another one."

"Ben, we don't need another fucking rock in front of the house, not to mention money is tight right now because I closed the business."

"No, I'm getting it. I'm getting a huge fucking boulder and I'm planting it right on the front lawn!" I said laughing hysterically. "You fuckers are never going to forget me. The boulder will be there long after I'm gone God forbid anything happens to me!" Nicole looked at me and her eyes welled up.

"You're an asshole," she said, shaking her head. "You're not going to die Ben." I looked over at her while I was driving taking my eyes off the road for a second.

"I'm getting the rock!" I said smiling.

We arrived at the Millstein Building and gave the car to the valet. This was one huge hospital, and the second time back I was more calm and aware of my surroundings. We entered the lobby where the limestone walls and cathedral ceilings seemed to go on forever. We checked in with security and were then directed to radiology for the CT scan. They stuck me with an I.V., pumped me with dye, and sent me through the ring on a platter just like last time. As I lay there, the seriousness of everything was weighing on me. I now fell into that category that you always hear other people gossiping about; people with serious health conditions that are subjected to a barrage of tests. Some of those stories I remembered didn't end too well. I tried not to think about the ones like my wife's co-worker who had a brain tumor at thirty-three and ended up having to have brain surgery. When I was finished with the CT scan we went upstairs to Dr. Stewart's office. Because of the technology, he would be able to pull up my CT scan in his office immediately. *God I hated hospitals. They made me shake inside.* I suppose it was from witnessing my brother go through five open heart surgeries from the time he was an infant to his most recent one at age twenty-nine. The doctors said his condition was not related to mine which was comforting, but not enough to quell my suspicion. He was born three months premature, blind, and with congenital heart defects. He had a hole in his heart, and a defective pulmonary valve.

My wife checked us in as we entered the waiting room in Dr. Stewart's office. While I was sitting there *Dr. Oz* passed by on his way out. *Holy shit, Dr. Oz! I just saw Dr. Oz from television pass in front of me. Very cool,* I thought. Dr. Mehmet Oz was in the same practice and hospital as Dr. Stewart. I had also read about another one of Dr. Stewart's colleagues, Dr. Craig Smith. He was the chairman of the cardiothoracic department and is also legendary in the field. I liked Dr. Stewart because he was in the same strata of surgeons, but also because he was passionate about aortic specific surgeries and he was young. I know it's silly, but something just didn't sit right with me about having an older surgeon. I figured the younger ones had to have steadier hands, better eyes, and more endurance. In my experience old people were usually set in their ways. I was afraid of getting a doctor that practiced the same old medicine and never changed with the times. Ridiculous or not, it frightened me; especially if I were going to be putting my life in their hands.

"Mr. Carey," a woman called from the desk. Debbie, Dr. Stewart's assistant greeted us. She is a small woman with dark hair and a sweet-as-pie manner. She brought us in the back to Dr. Stewart's office. As we walked in, the young man in the white coat stood up from behind the desk and extended his hand. This was Nicole's first time meeting him in person.

"I'm Allan Stewart," he said. We all shook hands. He has boyish good looks as my wife would say, and he resembles an NFL quarterback. I know she was expecting an old gray haired man, but this guy looked more like a Grey's Anatomy star. His hair was parted on the side, and he was all about business. He motioned for us to sit in the chairs across from his desk. We sat intently and he started typing at the keyboard.

"How big is it," I blurted out. He looked up for a second while typing and then turned the monitor on his desk so we could all see it.

"This is the CT scan that you just had twenty five minutes ago. The aneurysm is 6.3 centimeters. It's grown almost a full centimeter in six months."

My whole world caved in. *Fuck!* I thought. I turned my head to the side. I was so angry. Nicole's eyes welled up. I started dropping the business. "So what does this mean? When I went to see *Dr. X* six months ago he didn't seem to think I needed urgent attention. No disrespect doc, but doing open heart surgery for you guys is like changing your underwear, and I don't want to get cut open just because it's the textbook thing to do." I threw a copy of the aortic size vs. body size study from the medical journal in front of him. "What do you think of this?" I asked.

He started reading it and then he smiled and looked up. "One of the doctors that performed this study is my resident."

"Who?" I asked in amazement.

"Dr. Davies, he worked on this with Elefteriades at Yale. I'm going to call him up here so you can meet him."

"Really?" I laughed.

Dr. Stewart seemed amused by how excited I was. I zoned out as he dialed the phone. This was a day of Who's Who in doctors! I had read about all of these guys and it was very cool to be in the presence of such greatness. Dr. Stewart's voice interrupted my daydreaming. "He's in surgery now," he said as he hung up the phone. "I'm sure you'll get the chance to meet him. I am very familiar with that study."

"Doc, if you look at the study I'm not even in the high risk group! So what if I leave and don't do anything about the aneurysm right now?" I asked.

"You can, but Benjamin you have a family to think about," he said. You are living on borrowed time and you are going to have to deal with this at some point or you will die. Maybe you will be okay for a day, a week or a few months. No one knows the answer to that. I changed my whole practice as a result of a patient who died because of this condition. He had an aortic aneurysm that was 5.5 centimeters and we were planning surgery. I told him he shouldn't travel anywhere outside the proximity of a good heart center. He was overwhelmed by his diagnosis and thought his last days might be ahead. He went on a safari to Africa and died there of an untreated aortic dissection because there was no qualified medical help nearby."

I started asking a bunch of questions. "I'm a research freak and I've been diligent up to this point. What do you think about the *Ross Procedure*?" I asked.

"I don't," he said. "I've had to do some re-ops for complications resulting from *Ross's* and it's not pretty. It is a good procedure for children, and that is its limitation."

"Your *valve-sparing* procedure sounds incredible, and in my case would be perfect because there is nothing wrong with my valve. I don't need a valve replacement. Is this the *David Procedure?*" I asked. He looked amused with the street smarts I had acquired on my condition and the surgery. He was a good sport about it though and very patient.

"Not exactly," said Dr. Stewart, realizing that I was not the type that would be satisfied with generalities. "I've done many *valve-sparing* surgeries, and my method and technique resemble the *David Procedure*; however I've developed my own version of it over the years and have optimized it to yield the best possible results for my patients. I've had tremendous success." He threw a piece of white fabric tubing at me that looked like a mini vacuum hose. "This is what we replace the damaged portion of your aorta with. It's Dacron tubing."

My eyes bulged and I laughed. "Really? This big thing goes inside of me? Does it eventually turn into tissue?" I was intrigued, and I wanted to know every little detail of what this was about if I were seriously going to consider it. I asked Dr. Stewart dozens of questions over the next twenty minutes and he did not flinch once. He answered every question with articulate detail, and made me feel like he would stay another two hours if that's what it took to answer the questions to my satisfaction. The guy was amazing. My wife sat next to me the whole time smiling, probably happy that I was asking so many questions. In her mind if I was asking questions that was a good thing because it meant that I was finally surrendering to the idea of having the procedure done.

"Doc, I don't want to be ignorant about this, but if I'm not going to die tomorrow, then I'm not in a hurry to have this done. This is bad timing. Besides, what is my life going to be like after this? I don't want to have limitations, chronic pain, and a lower quality of life."

Dr. Stewart laughed. "You're a trip Benjamin. The risk of you having an aortic dissection with an aneurysm 6.3 centimeters and growing is greater than the risks associated with surgery. I have not lost a patient yet, I've had less than a one percent rate of infection, and less than ten percent of the patients have needed blood transfusions." He pulled a photo off the shelf next to his desk and handed it to me. "I replaced her aorta last summer. It was 5.3 centimeters, and she is doing great now." I smiled as I looked at the photo. The woman looked like a sports illustrated swimsuit model. She was wearing a yellow bikini, with oil glistening on her skin. Her scar after only six months looked barely noticeable. Now we were talking man to man. I felt like we should light up cigars on account of the picture. I looked over at Nicole with a smirk and she was shaking her head and rolling her eyes.

I turned back to Dr. Stewart. "This was your patient?" I asked. Dr. Stewart had already started dialing the telephone.

"Yes, I'm calling her right now so you can ask her any questions you might have."

I was surprised. "Okay, that's great!" I said.

When he got her on the telephone he explained the situation to her, and asked her to chat with me about her experience and answer any of my concerns. He handed me the phone.

"Hello," I said.

"Hello," a woman said, in a fine European accent. I smiled and we made small talk, and then I proceeded to ask her a list of questions about how she felt, whether she had any limitations, if the pain was bad, and if she remembered being on bypass. Putting me on the phone with a former patient was a great call on Dr. Stewart's part. It made me feel good to speak with someone who had a heart condition but wasn't a geriatric with clogged arteries from smoking and eating bad. It was silent for a moment after I hung up the phone and we all looked at each other. Dr. Stewart broke the silence.

"Benjamin, I can schedule you for surgery on Monday if you want."

"It's just not possible for me to have the surgery now. January would be much more ideal. Hypothetically though; if I were able to move forward with the surgery, could you do it right after the Halloween weekend?"

Nicole interrupted "Ben, he told you he could do it Monday, what's the point of waiting two more weeks? Just get it done now so we can all stop worrying."

"Nicole, there is no way in hell I'm getting this done on Monday. It probably won't be until January." She wasn't happy. She just looked at Dr. Stewart as if to say "See what I have to deal with?"

"I can schedule the surgery for Monday after Halloween Benjamin. That's November 2nd. Let me know what you decide, and don't hesitate to call me if you have any questions." He wrote on a yellow sticky pad, tore off the paper and handed it to me. "Call my cell."

We stood up and shook hands, and Nicole talked him up about his children on the way out. He had their pictures plastered all over the office and he lit up when he spoke about them. I was sorry to hear that he was *divorced. Who in their right mind would let him get away? I thought. Besides being a cool guy, he was the best aortic surgeon in the country; young, aggressive, and powerful. Money I'm sure wasn't a problem, and if you married a guy like that you had to know going into it that he wasn't going to be around. It seemed sad that someone lost out on getting to enjoy the finer parts of his mature career.* Then I had visions of him eating sushi in a hot nightclub, vodka tonic in hand, and ladies on each arm and I smiled. Maybe it wasn't so bad.

It was quiet all the way down the elevator and the entire time that we waited at the curb of the Millstein building for the valet to bring the car. Nicole and I were silent as we stared off in opposite directions. I felt bad that she had to go through this at five months pregnant. She must have felt terrified. On the drive home from Manhattan we spoke a little. "What are you going to do?" she asked.

"What do you mean what am I going to do?"

"Benjamin, you need to schedule the surgery."

"I'm not doing shit right now. You heard him; he said I could wait until January."

"No, that's what you wanted to hear, he didn't say that."

"Well I'm not getting it done right now. James just brought me into the company and we're launching a new website. I already closed one of the biggest finance companies in the country. You think I'm going to miss this new site going live?" Nicole shook her head and stared out the passenger window as if I weren't there. It started to rain, and with each sweep of the windshield wipers she faded away from me. She made a call to check on the kids and then it was quiet the rest of the ride home. We didn't talk or listen to the radio. We rode in silence except for the sound of the raindrops hitting the windshield, and the rhythm of the wipers going back and forth. Nicole rested her head against the raindrop covered window as trickles streamed down in random patterns.

The next week I resumed business as usual. By the end of the week my brother-in-law James pulled me into his office. He had probably heard about what transpired at the appointment from my wife. James and I had a good, but sometimes awkward relationship. He was about five years younger, but more successful. We had very different childhoods, were at different points in our lives, and I think sometimes we struggled to find commonality. In spite of that we respected each other from the day we met and had grown to care about each other like brothers. James has black hair with dark features and a pensive, articulate demeanor. Like me, the city had washed away anything suburban about his appearance.

He was wearing a black turtleneck, and a heavy steel Breitling wristwatch. I sat down across the desk from him.

"Dude what's going on with you? Is everything okay? How did your appointment go last week?"

"It went okay. Well; not really, but what can you do, ya know?"

"What do you mean? What did they say about the aneurysm?"

"Well, it grew from 5.3 centimeters to 6.3 centimeters in six months, and surgery is recommended for anything above five centimeters." I laughed, and he looked at me confused, not finding humor in anything I had said.

"That sounds serious, are you going to have surgery?" he asked.

I looked down at the floor and paused. "I don't know James. I really don't know what to do. What if I could live the rest of my life without having to have this surgery? I'm in great shape except for this stupid thing. Who even knows? I don't think I can handle this surgery. We're not talking about a little bypass surgery, or even a triple or quadruple bypass. We're talking about cutting off the main artery of my heart which supplies my entire body with oxygenated blood and replacing it with a hose. How the hell can I possibly ever be the same after that?" I had found that most people didn't know the magnitude of an aortic surgery. Everyone was accustomed to heart attacks and bypass surgeries, but not too many people were familiar with surgery for aortic aneurysms. An ascending aortic aneurysm like I had was at the base of the aorta right near the valve. Any cardiac surgery is serious, but to me the fact that they would be messing with the main line made it worse. I went on to explain to James what the operation would entail, how they would fix it, and I emailed him some videos of actual surgeries. He was analytical like me and I thought he would appreciate the videos.

"So what are you going to do?" he asked.

"Nothing right now. I'm going to help launch our new site and then worst case scenario I'll have the surgery in January when things slow down."

He gave me the puzzled look again. He looked me in the eye, and slowly leaned forward over the desk. "Ben let me tell you something; your well being is more important than anything. All of this will still be here if you have the surgery done now and come back. You have a key role here, and we have long term plans for you. Dave, Sung, and I have already spoken about this. Nothing will change for you here. Don't be an idiot. Get the surgery done now if that's what the doctor recommends. Why would you chance it?"

"I appreciate that James, I really do. I guess the truth is that I'm scared. I don't want my ribs sawed in half. I don't want to be hacked open like a deer, and disappear from the world for a few hours while they put me on bypass and then put humpty-dumpty back together again. I mean seriously, how can you ever be the same again after something like that? Where are you for the time your heart and breathing are stopped? These are not everyday things. Did you see those videos with the chest cavities open and veins popping out all over?" We both sat and just looked at each other. There was a brief silence. I think for the first time I had just admitted how I really felt out loud. James looked away with a smirk "Well Ben, if you put it like that I would be scared too, but you don't have much of a choice. Think about your family, you have a new baby coming. I would be more nervous walking around with that aneurysm in my chest than of having the surgery. Get it done. To be honest, now would be a better time anyway business-wise. I'm gonna need you in January. Anyway, don't let business be a factor in your decision. I want to be clear on that."

"I don't know what to say. I really appreciate the support James. You've just eliminated my last excuse." The ironic thing was that even though I felt overcome with gratitude after that conversation, I was more frightened than ever because I knew I was inching closer to the inevitable. I started to get up out of my chair. "I guess maybe I'll talk to Nicole and see if we can plan for a November 2nd surgery. We have an annual Halloween party for all the kids in the neighborhood and I don't want to have surgery before then and mess it up. I've been getting some sternum pain and shortness of breath though, so I suppose I can't escape this much longer."

James smiled and shook his head, "Do what you need to do and keep me posted," he said.

On the way home that evening I tried reaching out to my friend Jason, but he didn't answer. I had called him a few times over the past week or two, but he was missing in action. It bothered me because he knew I was having issues with my heart and facing a potential surgery. We had become distant over the past year because of some drama, and he was showing his true colors more and more. I was hoping to speak with him about what was going on in my life, and do some soul searching. I also knew I could count on his confidentiality. He was always a good listener and knew the right things to say to make you feel good. Our relationship was not as close anymore, but I never expected him to desert me. I let him stay in my apartment in the city for five years while he was going to film school, and got angry with him when he abruptly ditched the place to live with our friend Chris who had moved back to Manhattan. I should have known it would happen because he and Chris were like the *Odd Couple*. They were *Oscar and Felix* to a tee, and were growing into their late thirties having laid down no real roots to speak of. Jason didn't show an ounce of gratitude for what I did for him. He had the nerve to ask me for a couple hundred bucks to look after the place when he moved out, since he would still be living in the neighborhood. I would come to realize as a result of this event in my life, the depth of our true friendship. It's funny how that works. You spend your whole life with these images in your head of how your relationships are with people. As the years go by those relationships are tested, and only then do you realize their true nature. Only after they've been tested through weddings, moves, funerals, divorces, births, and other stages in life are you able to judge them. Until then, "best friend", "good guy", etc, are only labels. In the end, it's interesting; often surprising to see the results.

At home that evening Nicole and I had a heart-to-heart, and I told her I had decided to have the surgery on November 2nd. She started to give me a hard time about not getting it done sooner but realized she was wasting her breath. She seemed relieved, but I sensed that she was also sad. I could see pity in the way she looked at me; as if I were a flailing deer hit by a car and squirming in the road. I'm tough as nails, but my fear had become noticeable. "Yeah, let's have the big Halloween party like we do every year, and then I'll get this shit over with," I said. Her look of pity turned to laughter, and she gave me a big hug. I sighed.

The next day Nicole called and made the arrangements. My surgery was about a week and a half away. I spent the remaining days closing out business at work, tying up loose ends around the house, and preparing myself mentally. I thought about how I would feel on the day of surgery, and sometimes I started to go through the day in my mind. I could never imagine the whole procedure though. The whole ordeal was too much for me so I spent most of my time staying too busy to think about it. Any free time I had was spent with Nicole and the children doing intimate family things. We went pumpkin picking, raked leaves together, and walked along the pier in Northport Harbor watching the boats and the waves in the ocean. One of the most precious of these moments was me standing on the end of the pier holding the hands of my five year old daughter Milan, and my two year old son Preston. It was a rare moment of silence, and the three of us stood and looked out at the sailboats going up and down the choppy waves. As I watched the whitecaps on the waves, I thought of the new baby Nicole was carrying, and was going to give birth to in a few months. I hoped that nothing would happen during my heart surgery that would cheat me out of being there. I looked down to my left as the wind blew the curls on my daughter's hair, and a tear formed in my eye. I looked to my right and my son was resting his head against me. I took a deep breath and looked out to the horizon where the sky met the sea. At that moment I felt that no matter what happened I had experienced a richness that some men would never relish; not even in a lifetime. These last moments were bittersweet as we tried to cope with what was ahead. My five year old daughter Milan was old enough to realize what was going on, and too smart for us to hide it from her. This is a kid who is the youngest in her class and rarely brings home a test with a score of less than 100. She knew my heart was broken and had to be fixed by the doctor, and she demanded an explanation. I had to explain everything to her without being too graphic. I didn't want to frighten her, but I wanted her to realize the magnitude of the operation. I felt it was important for her to understand everything, in case God forbid something went wrong. Being candid with her also ensured that she would be helpful to Nicole instead of stressing her out. In regard to my two year old boy Preston; I just told him daddy's heart was broken and I was going into the hospital to get it fixed. I asked him to behave and help mommy as much as possible.

The following weekend we were on our way home from the grocery store and I pulled off the road abruptly.

"What are you doing?" asked Nicole as I pulled in to *Mother Earth*, our local landscape supply yard.

"I'm checking out boulders," I said smiling.

"You have to be kidding," she said. I put the truck in park quickly and jumped out of the truck smirking, slamming the door.

"I'll be quick," I shouted through the window, and she just looked at me annoyed. I went inside the office and saw the owner John at the counter. He was dirty from working in the yard, and he wore a baseball cap with his blonde hair sticking out the sides. John is one-hundred percent Irish and speaks with an accent. He and his family are very well liked in the community and they live around the corner from us. He had watched me transform my house from a ranch to a mansion, driving by every day during the construction offering compliments and advice. I had gotten thousands of pounds of wall stone from him to transform my landscape into a country oasis.

"What'll it be today?" asked John in his authentic accent.

"Hey buddy, how's it going? I'm looking for a huge boulder for landscaping. What do you have?"

"Did you check out some of those in the pile in the front?" he asked pointing to the pile of rocks near the entrance.

"Yeah, those aren't big enough. I need a huge one, like that one," I said, pointing to a six foot tall boulder that was part of the supply yard landscaping and not for sale. John smiled.

"Okay, well go around back and you'll find something like that. Here's a piece of chalk. They're in the four hundred dollar price range. Put a dot on the one you want."

"Okay John, thanks," I said, and I walked back out into the supply yard and around back. There were about seven huge boulders, and I immediately laid eyes on the one I wanted. It was a huge elongated boulder, almost as tall as I was and had contrasting tones of burnished copper, brown, and beige. I giggled inside. *This fucker would be around forever, and serve as a reminder to everyone of the blood, sweat, and tears I put into that house. Even if I died, my spirit would live on in that rock. Big, Obnoxious, and Enduring. One side of the stone was flat; perfect for a memorial plaque,* I thought. I ran back inside the office excited. John was still at the counter and I handed my credit card to him.

"I marked the boulder I want. I'm having open heart surgery next month, and I'm going to put that big ass rock right on my front lawn just in case," I said laughing. John seemed a little confused, but nodded as if he understood. He had to have been thinking what a crazy bastard I was. "I'm going to need it delivered tomorrow. Can you do that?"

"Sure," he said. "No problem. We're going to have to drive it over there by tractor if you want us to place it properly. If we do it by truck we'll just dump it and it will have to stay where it lands. I recommend we bring it by tractor so that we can move it around a bit and place it exactly how you want it."

"Okay John, sounds good to me. Can you bring it to my house tomorrow at around 11:30 a.m.?"

"Okay Benjamin," he said in his Irish accent.

I laughed mischievously, thanked him, and jumped back into the truck with Nicole and the kids feeling great about it!

"Did you get one" asked Nicole.

"What?" I asked.

"A rock Benjamin!"

"Oh. Not really," I said. "I saw a couple I liked. I'm definitely going to get one though. I'll probably do it next week." I didn't tell her it was coming the next day. I figured I would surprise her, and of course postpone the argument and lecture about spending four hundred bucks on a rock!

The next day Nicole and the kids left the house at around 10:00 a.m. because Milan had a soccer game. I stayed home to rake some leaves and wait for the delivery of the rock. I stood in the front yard with my rake, sipping on my morning coffee and watching the neighborhood slowly come alive. The Tallmans across the street came out and got in the truck with the kids, probably off to run errands. The door opened at the Pedersens next door and Erik and his two young sons came out with hockey equipment and took off in their car. Down the block two of my other neighbors stood at the foot of their driveways chatting in typical animated fashion. My other next door neighbor Mr. Hasenzahl came out to get his morning paper. "Mr. H." as I called him is a kind old widower from the old school. He was in his eighties. He went to church every Sunday, ate meat and potatoes, and had breakfast, lunch, and dinner every day at 8:00 a.m., Noon, and 5:00 p.m. like clockwork. He made his way cautiously down his front steps moving in slow motion as old people do, down the driveway to get the paper.

"Hey Mr. H. how ya doing?" He looked around in a daze and then focused on me standing in the front yard.

"Oh hi Ben. Take a day off would ya? What are you up to now?" he asked, alluding to the hundreds of projects he had seen me do, including some that really amused him. One time he watched in disbelief as I laid seven pallets of wall stone with my bare hands; working dawn to dusk, and setting up halogen lights so I could work until midnight for seven consecutive weekends.

"Not much, just doing some yard work," I replied. I wasn't about to tell him that my biggest fears were about to be delivered, manifested as an obnoxious five thousand pound, four hundred dollar memorial stone to be placed on my front lawn by a tractor!

"Well don't work too hard," he said, as he hobbled back up the driveway.

"No, not me."

I smiled. He went back inside and it was quiet except for the rustle of leaves in the trees and a couple random ones scuffling across the road. The sun shone brightly casting scattered rays through the trees. In the distance a deep motor cut through the serenity. I stood there in the front yard looking around to see if anyone was outside to witness the spectacle about to go down. Within moments the sound was so loud it shook the ground and a huge yellow bucket loader was blazing around the corner in a dust cloud and headed up the block. *Holy shit!* I thought, and I laughed out loud. People had to have run to their windows when they heard the commotion. It was a sight to see. The rock in the bucket was so heavy that it caused the tractor to bounce intermittently as it approached.

"Over here!" I directed John where to drop it like a flight coordinator. The tractor bucked and roared as we coordinated the perfect placement of the rock on the front lawn. A few moments later I signed off on the paperwork and the tractor drove off. It was quiet again as I took a step back and just stared. It was a serious moment, no longer amusing, as I stood there admiring the metaphorical rock. A smile returned to my face when I thought about what Nicole would think when she arrived home from the soccer game.

A couple of days later on a weeknight after work my friend Pete helped me move a six foot sofa into my apartment in the city. My mom and my wife were flipping out because they didn't want me lifting and carrying the heavy sofa up a five story walk-up, but I didn't give a shit. I needed the sofa out of my basement, and I thought it would be put to good use in the apartment in the city. I knew if I got cut open I wouldn't be moving anything for a long time so I wanted to get it done while I was still strong. My wife must have called up my mother the moment she heard my plan because the two of them harassed me relentlessly until I had the sofa loaded into the truck and they realized there was no stopping me.

Pete is about six feet tall and two hundred and forty pounds. He's a good looking guy of Greek descent, but he has a belly, a loud obnoxious mouth, and he's a chain smoker. A real *Morton Downey Jr.,* but my best and most trusted friend nonetheless. We didn't see each other much because we were both so busy, but we knew we could call on each other for anything. He was always there for me when I needed him, no matter what it was.

We had a typical drive into Manhattan laughing the whole way and catching up. Our lack of contact didn't change our friendship. *Quentin Tarantino* could have written the scene that ensued when we arrived at my building in the city and began unloading the sofa. Pete hopped out of the truck wearing a stretched out white t-shirt with his belly protruding; mesh gym shorts, and *Timberland* work boots. He lit up a cigarette and it never left his mouth or hand while we unloaded the sofa from the truck; nor did it while we struggled through the two glass entrance doors and up five flights of steep stairs. It was 11:30 p.m. by the time we entered the building, and I don't know what was more noisy; the sofa banging the walls as we carried it up, or our laughing and grunting the whole way.

"Come on you fuck!" Pete growled as the sofa got wedged making the corner on the third floor. The cigarette wiggled up and down in his mouth as he spoke. We paused for a moment and I looked down at him and burst into laughter. I laughed so hard that I let go of the sofa, and there he stood below me; both arms wrapped around it supporting all of the weight alone. He was beat red with the filthy cigarette hanging out of his mouth, sweat bullets on his forehead, and a cloud of smoke encircling him.

"Come on you fuck! What the fuck!" he grunted.

I laughed so hard tears came out of my eyes. I couldn't help him if I wanted to. Just seeing him steamed up cursing below me with the whole fucking sofa in his arms was like a cartoon! Finally I got my composure.

"Shhhhhh," I said. "There's fucking people sleeping. The fucking super is going to come out if you're not quiet."

"Yeah, whatever you fucking asshole! This was a brilliant idea! I don't know how the fuck I let you talk me into this shit! Grab this thing and let's go or I'm fucking leaving it here and going to the bar around the corner to do shots!"

He had sweat stains under his pits, and the cigarette was almost down to the filter. I continued laughing, and we finally got the sofa into the apartment on the fifth floor. We were both soaked with sweat. I may have had an aneurysm, but I tossed that sofa around like I was invincible.

"Thanks man. I really appreciate your help."

"Fuck you!" Pete said smiling, as he lit up another cigarette.

Seventy-Five percent of the time Pete and I spent together was spent laughing until our stomachs hurt. I cherished our friendship and would do anything for him in return. By the time we got back home that night it was about 2:30 in the morning, and Nicole was waiting up for me. She wasn't happy that I risked popping the balloon in my chest for a sofa, and she bawled me out. Denial is a strong thing, something that can easily hijack your judgment.

Halloween weekend arrived, and it was the last two days before my surgery. My family had come from four hours away to spend Halloween, see me through the surgery, and help my wife. Even my sister came down with her family, and that meant a lot to me. We had a few arguments over the past year and were just getting back on stable ground. Halloween fell on a Saturday, and it was a blast. Our whole neighborhood got together for trick-or-treating with the kids, followed by our annual tradition of a bonfire and outdoor movies. It was something everyone looked forward to each year. Every year a different family on the block would host the event, and this year it was our turn. People thought I was crazy for wanting such chaos at our place a couple of days before the big event; but it actually kept my mind off things and I wouldn't have had it any other way. Nicole and I were dressed up as pirates, and for a few hours it felt good to be someone other than the guy with the aneurysm. I got a chance to catch up with the people dearest to me, and seeing the kids have such a blast was exactly what I needed to keep my spirits up. I wanted to stay busy, not sit around and mope.

Maybe I was just being paranoid and self conscious; but I felt like people at the party were looking at me in pity and thinking, *Oh that poor bastard*. I started thinking that if I made it through everything okay I was going to get right back into shape and flex my iron will. I was not going to let this event define me.

At the end of the night after everyone had left I started folding up chairs. It was a perfect fall night. The air was crisp, the sky was pitch black and dotted with stars, and the wind whispered through the trees rustling the dry leaves overhead. I leaned the chairs up against the porch, and sat down for a moment alone in front of the bonfire. I could feel my grandmother's presence as I stared into the orange and yellow flames. In a weird coincidence, I was going to be having my heart surgery on the exact day she died a couple of years ago. I didn't mention it to anyone, but others had to have realized; especially my Mom. I sat there in front of the fire and reflected on my last moments with my grandmother. I was alone by her bedside and held her hand when she drew her last breaths. She literally died in my arms. I remember that night as if it were yesterday. It was my first and only experience losing someone I was close to, at an age where I knew what was going on. I concluded that my grandmother would be watching over me during the surgery. I watched the coals smolder, and the heat felt good on that cold October night. For a moment I felt like everything was going to be okay. I was terrified, but I had finally come to accept it. I stood up and put my hands in my pockets. I turned toward the house and each window was lit up because I had so many relatives staying with us. It was pretty, and it reminded me of that big house on that old 80's sitcom *The Waltons*. Even the *dog-houses*, and *eyebrow windows* were lit up because my sister was staying on the third floor. I smiled as I watched my kids and my nephews go from window to window running back and forth chasing each other and wrestling. In the kitchen windows I could see my mom and mother-in law leaning over the counter talking. Then our big mahogany front door opened and Nicole called from the porch, "Ben, come inside!"

"I'll be right in," I said. I turned back to the glowing red coals in the fire. Then I turned my attention to the strong wind blowing through the leaves on the elm trees above. I took one last soulful look up at the sky. It was crystal clear with a full moon. I sighed as I got up from the chair and went inside; enjoying the company of everyone for the rest of the night. I had a chance to chat with my brother and sister until the wee hours of the morning. My brother was a pillar of strength having been born blind and having five previous open heart surgeries of his own. He didn't have to say or do anything. His presence alone was a reminder of how resilient the human spirit is. I went to bed that night and slept sound like a baby. *Goodnight Ben, Goodnight Erin.*

The next morning I slept late, and spent the day with my family having the same intimate conversations, laughing, reminiscing and trying not to think about what I was about to go through the next day. Nicole's mom came over for dinner, and gave me Ralph Lauren pajamas to wear during my recovery. It was a cute gesture. We had come a long way despite some differences in the past, and we finally had an understanding and appreciation for each other.

Sunday night Nicole rallied the troops. Thank God for her. "The kids need to be in bed by 7:00 p.m. every night," she told both of our moms who were seated at the table with her. She checked off items on a sheet and our mother's looked at her like she was crazy. They didn't dare say anything though. "Milan needs to be up by 7:00 a.m., and they are not allowed to have junk food or watch cartoons during the week." She proceeded to brief them on a full week at the Carey compound, since they would be running it while I was in the hospital. Nicole was insisting on being at my side every second until I returned home. We had ups and downs in our marriage, but I could not have married a more dedicated woman. She arranged everything so that no one would miss a beat during our absence. My wife is feisty, something I loathe and adore at the same time. No one dared question her. I don't know what I would have done without her, or without the help of our mothers. Later Nicole went through a similar routine with me upstairs, "Okay, did you pack your Ipod? Your slippers?" I laughed at her as she went down the list because I didn't need the drilling, I was all set.

"Let's just go to sleep before I change my mind about this!" I laughed. I put our packed bags by the front door, and said goodnight to everyone staying at our house. Then I went and gave each of the kids a kiss goodnight, and went to bed myself. We had to leave at 4:00 a.m. to be at the hospital for the pre-surgery screening. We had a close group of friends in the neighborhood and one of them, Danielle, had offered to get up and drive us into the city so that we didn't have to fuss with parking a car for the duration of my stay. We were blessed to be in the company of such good friends and family. I slept soundly again that night.

I woke up at 3:20 a.m. without an alarm clock. I have no idea why, but I fell back asleep.

"Beep, beep!" a horn blared.

I looked over at the clock and it was 4:10 a.m. I jumped out of bed feeling frazzled and ran over to the window. Danielle was out front in her truck waiting for us. It was dark and cold and wisps of exhaust rose from the back of the truck. Nicole got up behind me and started a typical frenzy.

"Oh my God! It's Danielle! We overslept!" I stood there sleepy, scratching my belly and laughing.

"Oh well. They can't do the surgery without me," I said. Nicole paused, looking at me with piercing eyes; then made a bee line for the bathroom. I followed Sergeant Carey and jumped in the shower to wash my body with the special soap the hospital had prescribed. As I toweled off in the bedroom, the dimness and silence of the house hit me. I was in that foggy, middle of the night state-of-mind. I put on a sweat suit and slippers and could not stop thinking that this was just a bad dream. You could have heard a pin drop. It felt like the twilight zone.

"Ben!" Nicole startled me, and I was brought back to reality. "We have to leave!" I went in to kiss each of my kids goodbye. Milan, my five year old lay with the blankets kicked off and her long beautiful hair spilled out all over the pillow. My two year old Preston also lay with the blankets off; his mouth wide open as if catching flies and his eyebrows squinted with a look of concentration. It was priceless and made me laugh. I rushed downstairs and we left in the dark.

The sun was rising by the time we arrived at the Millstein building in Manhattan. We said farewell to Danielle and then went inside to check in. The hospital was already bustling at 5:30 a.m. Nicole and I proceeded to the pre-surgery waiting room. We waited for what seemed like an eternity and then we were finally called to have baseline readings taken and answer a series of questions. I sized up the patients around me, wondering what they were there for. I didn't say much to the nurses or anyone else. I was nervous. Even my conversation with Nicole consisted of only short responses to her questions. I could not believe that in a matter of minutes I would be lying on an operating table with a circular saw blade burning through my ribs. I was shitting bricks. My parents, sister and brother arrived and spent the last twenty minutes waiting with us. Then at about 6:45 a.m. a nurse called us up to the front desk of the waiting room. She said she was going to bring us upstairs to the cardiothoracic surgery wing of the hospital. "We'll stay here," said my stepdad Ed. Ed has short brown curly hair and a beard. He carries himself with visible confidence and stature, qualities ascribed to his success in the business world. I could tell today though that there was a slowness to his swagger, and he was upset. He had basically raised me with my mom, and it wasn't easy for him to see me in such a vulnerable position. I gave him and my brother a hug, and then Nicole, my mom, and my sister went upstairs with me. It was quiet in the elevator, and I began fidgeting nervously. There was something grossly barbaric about knowing what was about to take place, and the instinctual reactions happening with my body. We got off the elevator and were led to a series of three-sided cubicles, apparently the holding pens for the patients undergoing open heart surgery. Everything was bright and immaculate, and the place was lit up like Times Square on New Year's Eve. We were greeted by a friendly nurse, and introduced to the anesthesiologist and a few other techs. They were all in good spirits, and very nice. "Where is Dr. Stewart?" I asked nervously.

"He'll be here shortly," one of the nurses said. She handed me a gown and asked me to take everything off and put it on. I hid behind the curtain and put the gown on. When I was finished I sat down in a chair in the cubicle. My mom, sister and Nicole stood because there was no place else to sit. The anesthesiologist crouched down in front of me like a coach and began telling me what the next steps were.

"Dr. Stewart will be here momentarily to say hi. Shortly after that I will bring you to the operating room, where you will lie down and listen to relaxing music. The team will begin prepping you. You will be given I.V.'s in each arm and we will administer the initial anesthesia after the second I.V. is put in. You should not remember anything after that. You will wake up in recovery and be on your road to healing up."

"Can you give me the anesthesia after the first I.V.? I hate needles. I don't want to be awake for anything."

"Normally we don't administer anything until both I.V.'s are in, but, we can do that if Dr. Stewart is okay with it."

"Thanks, I appreciate it."

As we finished chatting, Dr. Stewart arrived. He was dressed like Patrick Riley ready for a Knicks game. He wore an expensive suit, and had a thick Windsor knot in his tie with a perfect crease. I had perfected the Windsor, and in my opinion a good one said a lot about a man. Most guys were still lobbing up those lopsided grade school knots. He looked bubbly and refreshed for 6:30 in the morning, and had another doctor standing next to him in a white lab coat.

"This is Dr. Davies," said Dr. Stewart. "He will be assisting me in your surgery."

Dr. Davies was the doctor behind the medical journal study on aorta size that I was so familiar with. I was surprised to meet him. He is a lot bigger than I imagined. He is imposing and easily over six feet tall.

"It's an honor to meet you Dr. Davies," I said, shaking his hand. Dr. Stewart stepped aside to talk with the anesthesiologist, and I began chatting up Dr. Davies. "So Dr. Davies, do you really think I need this surgery?" He looked at me like he couldn't believe I had the balls to ask the question at that moment.

"Yes," said Dr. Davies, smirking and noticeably uncomfortable that I was brazen enough to ask this in front of Dr. Stewart.

"Really? Even in spite of that study you worked on that I read about regarding aortic size vs. body size?"

"Yes, there were a lot of variables in that study. Your aorta is over 6 centimeters, and you are at risk."

Dr. Stewart came back over. "Doc, no one else will be operating on me except you right?" I asked. If Dr. Davies was uncomfortable with the last conversation, he was even more so now. I didn't give two shits who I offended. This was my life and death moment and I needed to make sure everything was in check. They both smiled at me, and then Dr. Stewart got serious.

"I will be the only one operating on you. Dr. Davies may hold a stitch while I tie, and assist, but I will be performing every last procedure." Dr. Stewart was very serious and candid about that, and it made me feel good. Whether he was telling the truth or not, it's what I wanted to hear. I was terrified of having this procedure right up until I went into the operating room, but I was confident that I had the best surgeon in the world working on me. It was a celebrity team I had researched and read about, and I was in the same place that President Clinton came to for open heart surgery a few months prior. Money couldn't buy a better doctor, team or hospital, and I felt great about that. I couldn't comprehend an operation of this magnitude at a run of the mill suburban hospital with a bypass surgeon who might see one or two of these aortic cases in a year.

"I'm going to get changed and prepared," said Dr. Stewart. "Spend a few moments with your family, and then the team will take you to the operating room to get you ready. You are going to be fine Benjamin, and you'll be around for many years to come."

"Really? I just walk to the operating room and hop on the table? I figured I would be asleep when you brought me in there. No stretcher or anything?"

"No, the operating room is right over there," and he pointed to a hinged door with a small tinted porthole.

I laughed nervously, "Okay." With that, he put his hand on my shoulder and then swaggered away like Patrick Riley ready to kick in the doors to the Garden for the finals.

I turned to Nicole, my mom, and sister. My mom hugged me. "Okay, I guess this is it," she said.

"Wait, you don't have to leave yet," I said, my heart beating out of my chest. The nurse looked at us both and nodded her head affirmatively as if to say it's time.

"We'll let you guys say goodbye," my mom said, leaving Nicole and I for a last moment.

My sister hugged me and said "You'll be okay," but she was pale and serious. It was painful for her to witness because of my big ego. It was the epitome of vulnerability.

They left and Nicole stared at me. I looked down, not wanting to make eye contact with her for fear of a breakdown. I looked at the little medal of the Virgin Mary that my mother had pinned to my medical wristband. When my Nana was alive she had it blessed by the Pope, and insisted my brother wear it for his open heart surgery. After she passed my brother went on to wear it for five more open heart surgeries. As I fiddled nervously with the medal I asked God one final time to watch over me so that I could stick around for my family. I was more nervous about breaking my daughter's heart than I was afraid of dying. She was old enough to know what was going on, and I didn't want to traumatize her and leave her with emotional baggage by keeling over at such a young age.

I looked up at Nicole. "Holy shit! Here we go right? I'm really doing this?"

"Yes, it's for the best. You'll die if you don't." She put my hand on her belly. "We have a baby coming, and I need you to be strong, and be here with us."

I nodded my head. "If anything happens to me, make sure you hang on to the house, and you can name the baby Benjamin if it's a boy." We both laughed. We didn't know the gender of the baby, but I knew in my heart it was a boy. Nicole wanted to name him Benjamin, but I didn't want a junior. The house was something I had put every ounce of my blood, sweat, and tears into and I wanted it to live on in my legacy as well.

"You're nuts," she laughed. We held each other for a moment and then the nurse summoned me.

"Okay Mr. Carey we're ready for you." We both took deep breaths and let go. Nicole looked sad and slowly walked away watching me. I acknowledged the nurse and began to follow her across the hall to the waiting room as Nicole and I waved goodbye. I walked slowly alongside the nurse, my gown waving loosely in the back and then "thump"; as quick as a strike on a bass drum I was utterly and completely alone with strangers, about to be dissected. She pushed the door open to the waiting room and ultra bright light escaped. Inside, everything was bright and whitewashed with dozens of high tech machines, wires, and video screens. It resembled what I thought the inside of a UFO would look like. In the center of the room there was an operating table surrounded by a bunch of doctors and nurses laying out tools and preparing for God only knew what was about to go down. The table itself was high like an ironing board, and no larger than a human body. It was probably designed that way to support the body, while simultaneously allowing doctors unobstructed maneuvering and full access. It looked like an uncomfortable pedestal; a focal point to which all attention would be focused on shortly. The spotlights on it were even brighter than the rest of the lights and beamed down on it illuminating it like a prize. I stood there in awe and at that point could not wait to be knocked out. There was no more fear, just a desire to get drugs in me as soon as possible. The nurse walked me over to the operating table and I got up on it. The anesthesiologist I had met earlier was seated near the table, probably putting the final touches on the drug cocktails. He smiled and we exchanged hellos as I climbed onto the table.

"You're going to knock me out after the first I.V. right doc?" I asked him.

"Yes," he smiled.

"Great," I said as the nurses covered me with heated blankets. One of the nurses asked me for my signature and approval for a medical equipment company rep. to observe the surgery. I was not alarmed about it, as I had heard from my friend Ken who had a similar surgery that this was common.

"Mr. Carey," said one of the nurses in an Indian accent. "We are going to start the I.V., and after we begin administering the drugs you will become drowsy. We will be inserting a *Swans* catheter in your neck and a urinary catheter and preparing you for surgery. Once the medication is started however you won't remember much." I lay there zoned out while she was talking looking up at the sea of lights and wires above me. *How did I get here? I wondered. How did this happen? Am I going to make it?* I prayed to God, and prayed for my wife and kids. I felt the nurse reaching for my right arm.

"You're going to feel a pinch," she said in her Indian accent. She was very sweet. They all were. Dr. Stewart arrived, and I heard him interrogating everyone with the standard checks and balances. Then he came over and placed his hand in mine like a football coach and squeezed.

"Are you ready?" he asked.

"Yes," I mumbled groggily. The last thing I remember was the anesthesiologist asking me how I felt, and the nurse putting the urinary catheter in. On a normal basis it would be excruciatingly painful, however at this point I was high as a kite. After that I lay there in a fog, barely conscious. I could hear voices growing fainter, and then I don't remember anything. Below is a journal Nicole kept of what transpired while I was under:

7:22 a.m. - *They just took you into the operating room. The anticipation.*

8:45 a.m. - *I wonder if they have you prepped yet. There is silence in the waiting room. This is not a happy place. Families are waiting here, looking eagerly at the door every time they hear a noise, hoping that it is a nurse or the doctor to tell them good news. I am sitting here hoping that I have told you enough, loved you enough. I mean the "what if" factor is screaming in my head. I hate it. People handle stress differently. Ed had to eat. I needed to cry. We made jokes about your grandma. She passed away today three years ago. This is why I know you're not going anywhere. She's protecting you. This date is no coincidence. I wonder if you're sleeping already, where do you go when you're unconscious. Would you see pop ?*

9:50 a.m. - *No word on your status yet. My stomach is in knots. A couple of families have been relieved of their wait, but not me. Thoughts race through my mind. I couldn't fathom life without you. Friends and family have been emailing and sending their prayers and I am grateful but they have no idea what the rest of forever feels like. Blink. It could all be different.*

10:05 a.m. - *My heart just stopped. A nurse came in and said, "Carey family?" You are on bypass now. She said your value is good and they will only have to replace the root and part of the aorta. Now the surgery begins. If you see me writing this; I love you.*

10:45 a.m. - *Dr Stewart walks into the waiting room. His facial expression brings relief. The procedure went well... you were lucky. If you waited any longer it would have ruptured. He gave you a month. The walls were paper thin.*

11:45 a.m. - *Waiting again to see you post op. They are holding you downstairs for an hour (which they say is normal) and I am waiting to see you. The relief is overwhelming.*

2:50 p.m. - *This is how long it has taken me to see you. (I keep on calling and seeing if something was wrong-no answers). You are sleeping. You did have some minor complications which I am trying to get to the bottom of. You afib'd prior to bypass and you have some excess bleeding from the chest tubes. I told your mom. I found this out by looking at your paperwork. Thank God I am OCD! She thinks it's nothing; I'm waiting to talk to Dr. Stewart. Seeing you there gave me a choking feeling. I hated it. I'm overwhelmed and tired and I feel I can't rest. Something doesn't seem right. I am going to see you again soon. I love you.*

3:45 p.m. - Just visited you again. You are getting some blood. I am waiting for Dr. Stewart.

5:30 p.m. - You opened your eyes and could squeeze my hand. You probably won't remember but that has been the best feeling all day. You are still bleeding more than they would like. They are giving you two bags of FFP, which is a blood product to help thicken the blood to promote clotting. You are on some insulin too. The communication between the nurses and myself has been wonderful, but if I did not ask questions, they would not offer any information. Still waiting for Stewart but he has been making all your medical calls from the O.R., he is working on another patient. I love you. The hardest part I thought was going to be the surgery. It is this that has been the most troublesome. I could only imagine how you would be if it was me. I am trying to be that person for you. We are connected souls, every time there is an issue, my soul knows. I will not rest until I know you are ok.

7:00 p.m. - Dr. Stewart finally came and spoke to me. He told me you afib'd before going on bypass prior to the surgery and that was not unusual. He told me you were doing well and that the bleeding was because you are a big man. He said you were stable. I hugged him and thanked him for saving your life today. He told me that if you didn't have the procedure done you would have been dead in a month. Divine intervention. I thank God for that.

8:00 p.m. - *I go in to see you and they tell me they needed to sedate you because you are bleeding again, more than they would like. Needless to say I am beyond frustrated and trying to remain positive. I mean, just an hour ago Stewart was talking like you'd be off the ventilator already. Your bloods should be back in an hour and I am going to check on you again.*

9:15 p.m. - *Went to check on you and they needed to give you more FFP (plasma). It seems to have stabilized you and they are going to try to take you off of sedation. The nurse is going to call me when I can see you again.*

11:15 p.m. - *Your eyes are open and you are here. Your breathing tube is out and for the first time in almost fifteen hours I feel relief. Your first words are how hot you are and how you feel like you have socks in your mouth because it is so dry. The overnight nurse pales in comparison to your afternoon nurses. I feel bad for any patient if they don't have family. You would think it would be the opposite.*

3:45 a.m. - *I come down to see you again. We talk. You want to know everything, which is how I know you are getting better. I don't blame you. I would want to know too. Every day is a gift they say, today was my gift for a lifetime. I decided while I awaited the unknown, that even though we aren't perfect individually, together we have things just right. Our individual quirks and imperfections although trying at times, really mean nothing in this vastness called life.*

5:45 a.m. - *I come to see you again, you play a smartass trick on me and ask me who I am. I wanted to beat you and then I was reminded again, just how quickly you were coming around. I'd much rather have it this way. I hold your hand and you feel at peace to rest. You tell me how horrible the nurse is. It reminds me of when pop used to complain. The nurses have actually been great, but you are miserable and I understand. I'm glad you are complaining, it means you are strong.*

11:00 a.m. - *They have moved you to a step-down room. You still have your chest tubes in, and you look really weak. Your mouth is white and so are your hands and feet. Your output isn't great but all in all you are moving along and staying positive. You are hysterical when you are drugged. You are so loopy. The nurse keeps asking me if you are in pain because you have used your pump ninety-six times and it is set to dispense only thirty-six -- a kid in a candy store. That's what it reminds me of.*

5:00 p.m. - You sat up today. You are so weak. It is scary. I'm nervous because something doesn't seem right. Still can't put my finger on it.

11:00 p.m. - I bring you soup and tiramisu, thinking that I will be able to feed you. You are sweet and you eat some soup so as not to disappoint me. I know you are tired though, and don't want to be bothered. You are so exhausted and you need rest, so I let you be.

4:00 a.m. - I race downstairs because I had a nightmare. You are there, eager to see me. You are fine. It was my mind playing tricks on me. I feed you some tiramisu and stay with you until 6:30 a.m. You fall back to rest. I go upstairs and just thank God you are here with me.

10:00 a.m. - The kids are coming to see you soon.

I vaguely remember my Uncle Tye and Brennan's loud boisterous voices when I first came out of surgery and was still on the breathing tube. They are loud and Irish and they supposedly had everyone in the room laughing! Tye is an iron worker and Brennan is a mason. They both have loud distinct voices and their conversation was commonly sprinkled with a nice mix of humorous slang and profanities. There were four more of them and any time two or more of my uncles got together it was a recipe for gut busting laughter. My mom says that they were making fun of my black toenail that I had dropped a brick on working around the house a week before surgery. They were making jokes about it and cracking on me.

It was comforting to hear them, and flattering that they traveled five hours just to see me for an hour and show me love. That's what we did in my family. At the drop of a dime we were there for each other in times of crisis.

My first vivid memory after surgery was having the breathing tube pulled out. I remember the nurse saying "Okay Mr. Carey, you're doing great! We are going to take out your breathing tube. I need you to exhale when I pull the tube out." As she pulled it out mucus was suctioned out of my lungs and throat and it was disgusting. I exhaled, and coughed up phlegm. Once it was out I coughed a little more, and began breathing on my own. I immediately had a sensation of heat, and extreme dryness in my mouth. It felt like a ball of hot socks was stuffed in there. I started groaning, and it got the ICU nurses attention and she put her ear near my mouth.

"I'm thirsty," I grunted, in my drunken state.

"I can't give you any water Mr. Carey, it will make you nauseous."

"My mouth is dry," I said.

"Let me rinse you," said the nurse. She then took what felt like a mini wet sponge on a stick and wiped the inside of my cheeks, my tongue, and the roof of my mouth. I felt like I was in heaven. It was one of the most quenching and refreshing feelings I've ever had. I was so parched and dry, and the wet sponge wiped away the mucus and hydrated my mouth. That little wet sponge on a stick felt like a miracle; an oasis in a desert. A short time after that I had conned the nurse into giving me ice chips which she warned would make me nauseous. They felt like fireworks; exploding, and melting into ice cold water when they hit my tongue. Because my mouth was like an inferno, the water evaporated immediately. It was amazing, but within a few minutes of eating them I got a severe case of nausea. I felt like I was going to throw up all over and the nurse had to give me some anti-nausea medicine.

I was in a fog. I couldn't see anything, I was just there, existing in a haze. I just lie there, taking in information from my sense of touch and hearing, but not sight. It was a combination of the drugs and trauma to my body that reduced me to that state. I remember Nicole coming in and putting her hand on my forehead, kissing me and hugging me, and then interrogating the nurses. I loved her and was happy to see her. There was no question with her on duty that anything would get overlooked. She was my soldier, and I knew she was capable of running the Carey family in my absence if it came down to it. She reminded me of my mother in many ways. She loved deeply but had a combative nature that you didn't want to summon. She was also a hard worker and would carry the weight of the world for someone she loved. She slept at the hospital, and I remember her coming back to see me in ICU every moment that they would let her. I wanted to get the hell out of there, but she told me I had lost a lot of blood and they were working on stabilizing me before they would move me. I was so out of it. I could care less about anything. I just lay there like a zombie waiting for my soul to re-inflate like a blowup doll. Surprisingly, the pain was nothing like I expected. The worst part of the surgery was the extreme dry-mouth I felt after they pulled the breathing tube out. I didn't feel any pain in my sternum thanks to the morphine. Before surgery, my biggest fear was that I would wake up feeling the pain and wrath of being sawed in half like one of those magic show acts. I wondered how it was possible for me to be so comfortable after surgery. They had sawed through my sternum bone and spread my ribs with clamps to hold them open for hours while they worked on me, yet I didn't feel any pain.

It turns out I had to have a blood transfusion after surgery as a result of excess bleeding. In my consultation before surgery, Dr. Stewart had told us this was something with low probability. It ended up happening to me, and I was pissed off about it. I was adamant about not wanting anyone else's blood and the excess bleeding turned out to be one of the most significant obstacles for me. I had a low red blood count for quite a few weeks after surgery, and it made me feel like a zombie. My skin and fingernail beds were snow white, and I couldn't think straight. I looked like the kid in the movie *Powder*. I had absolutely no energy, and my memory was horrible. It took longer than expected for my blood levels to stabilize. It got so bad at one point that I almost had to have a second blood transfusion. I was afraid of having more strange blood dumped in me. Life to me is so much more than what we see on the outside. I had done a lot of reading in the past on "cellular consciousness", and it caused me to feel uncomfortable with the idea of someone else's life being injected into me. Two of the best books I ever read were *The Biology of Belief* by Bruce Lipton and *The Secret of Water* by Masaru Emoto. These books isolated the cellular unit of life and scientifically explained how our bodies are merely collective representations of our smaller units of life; our cells. On the verge of needing another transfusion Dr. Stewart decided against it because he was confident that I would respond on my own. He felt that I was young enough to recover without intervention. All I know is that I felt like complete shit. They ended up giving me FFP which I was told is one of the components of your blood. The nursing staff was incredible. They were constantly testing my levels and administering drugs and blood to keep me out of the black hole. I was delirious and felt like a science project. They were in my face every few minutes, and all I could do was keep pressing the button on the joystick they gave me to automatically administer morphine. At one point the nurse came in smiling and asked me, "How is your pain?"

I looked up dazed and confused. "I'm okay," I said. She kept smiling and standing there. "Why?" I asked.

"Well because the morphine is set to only deliver thirty-six doses, but it records every time that you press the button. You pressed the button ninety-six times," she said. I laughed deliriously.

"Oh," I said. "I guess that's par for the course with me," and we both laughed.

My children came to see me. My mother-in-law brought them in, and I could hear them coming down the hall ahead of her before they even made it into the room. I was exhausted, but I smiled when I heard their voices. Milan came into the room first with Preston trying to elbow his way ahead of her. "Hi daddy," they both said.

"Hi guys."

I looked at them and smiled. It was awkward. I hated that they had to see me so weak. At first they were overwhelmed with the whole scene in front of them. Both of their eyes scanned the room and everything in it. They looked up at the monitors, at the I.V's in my wrists, and all of the wires and tubes connected to me. Milan seemed upset about how I looked, and Preston was dead serious about everything. He looked at the I.V., and then at my face, at the monitor, and then at my face. He continued to do this in rapid succession for about two or three minutes, and then he finally asked, "Daddy, are you okay?"

"Yeah, I'm okay buddy. Daddy is okay. They fixed me up, now I just need to get better so I can come home." With that Preston jumped up on the bed with me, causing Nicole to get anxious about all the wires and tubes connected to me.

"It's okay honey. Don't worry about it."

I hugged my little boy, and Milan came to my side and gave me a big hug. I let go first and they were still hugging me so I continued to hug them back. It may have been our longest hug ever. I looked up.

"You're still in one piece!" I said to my mother-in-law. She smiled at me.

"Yeah, they didn't break me yet!"

"Thanks for all of your help with everything mom, I really appreciate it."

"It's nothing," she said. "Just do what they tell you so we can get you home and help you get better."

"Thanks," I said, trying to manage a smile.

They didn't stay too long. After about a half-hour Preston was bored, and had started poking around to see what was up with my roommates. Nicole decided it was probably time for them to go before he started unplugging them. I was nearly asleep when they left and struggled to give them hugs goodbye. I promised them I would see them soon, and my mother-in-law took them back home.

Over the next few days my body slowly and stubbornly responded and came to a fragile stability. I felt a lot of love while I was at the hospital. I was touched by the number of friends and family that took time out of their busy work week to come by and say hello to me. Some of them came late at night after work because it was the only time they had. It was nice, and it gave me strength. My mom would stay with Nicole and me at the hospital, and then go back to our house to help my mother-in-law take care of the kids. I was in ICU for a couple of days and then they brought me to the CCU unit which was a step down. When I arrived in CCU, the nurses gave me a nice reception and were flirting with me. They made jokes about their colleague, a hot blonde who would be caring for me. Thank God for those friendly and nurturing nurses. They treated me as if they genuinely cared about me, and spoke to me like a friend would. They were amazing people, and their down to earth mentality, jokes, and ability to put a positive twist on everything was what got me through each day. Every time I fell asleep, I would be awakened by shots of heparin in my stomach, blood tests, drug dispensing and other unpleasant things. It was non-stop. I was in a room with three other patients. Two of them looked to be in their seventies, and the man next to me on the other side of the curtain was in his forties and just had a complete heart transplant. We were all battling our own demons, so there wasn't much conversation; just a lot of ungodly sounds. I spoke a little with the man next to me. We joked with each other about our conditions but also offered each other encouragement. I heard the poor guy being put through test, after test, after grueling test on the other side of the curtain; his wife at his side the whole time. He had all sorts of tests; spinal taps, biopsies, blood tests, you name it. I would hear the doctors tell him and his wife about each of these tests, and listening to their reaction was heartbreaking. I felt so bad for both of them. They were both very positive though, and the man took it like a champ. Each time they came to give him a test, or wheeled him out for one of those tortuous procedures I thought of how lucky and fortunate I was. He gave me strength.

A day or two after surgery a nurse came to take out my urinary catheter. I was so complacent and out of it that I hadn't really given it much notice. The nurse was a laid back and down to earth dark skinned woman.

"Mr. Carey," she said, in a west-indies accent. "We are going to remove your urinary catheter now." I looked down at the bag of piss as if noticing it for the first time and gasped.

"Oh that's just great," I said.

"Now now Mr. Carey, you won't feel much. It's okay."

"Just get it over with," I said. I closed my eyes and tried to block out any vision of what was going on. A few deep breaths and loud growls later it was out. It was over in an instant, but the anxiety caused sweat beads on my forehead. *Thank God that's over,* I thought.

"We'll be taking out your chest tubes tomorrow," said the woman.

"Oh my God," I said, half laughing. "I can't wait!"

"You'll be okay," she said. "You will feel better when the tubes come out, and be on your way to going home."

I hadn't seen my scar or chest tubes. I didn't have the stomach for it, and I wanted to see as little as possible. I peeked under my gown and saw that the chest tubes were basically two pieces of clear latex tubing that stuck out of my torso right at the bottom of my ribs. I was surprised at how large the tubes were. They were about the diameter of one of my fingers. The tubes went into my chest cavity to allow any excess blood and fluid to drain out after they closed me up. According to the nurse, the idea was to leave them in long enough to drain the fluids, but not long enough to precipitate any infection. The timing of their removal seemed like a big deal to the doctors and nurses. I was dreading having them removed.

The next day my favorite nurse with short blonde hair woke me up. She is very petite with blue eyes and a great personality complementing her looks. She was my *Sleepless in Seattle*. "Hi there. I'm going to take out your chest tubes today," she said. I was not happy, but I figured at least they sent the right person to do it. I sobered up quick.

"Really?"

"Yes. This will only take a second."

"Is it going to be painful?" I asked.

"You might feel a little pain, but overall you will feel more comfortable when they are out."

"Let's just do it quick," I said. The nurse pulled aside my gown and located the tubes with her fingers.

"Okay Mr. Carey, I'm going to put some pressure near the tubes with one hand and pull them both out at the same time with the other. There are also two tiny wires that I need to pull out."

"Wait a second! What are the wires for? I didn't know there were wires in there too!"

"Yes Mr. Carey the wires were left inside of you in case your heartbeat malfunctioned and needed to be shocked back into normal sinus rhythm. I'll forewarn you though; sometimes they get a little stuck because they start to attach themselves as you heal, so you might feel some light tugging when they come out."

"Are you serious?" I asked.

"Yes, now are you ready?" She had lowered the bed all the way down and stood leaning over me, positioned to pull out the tubes.

"Holy shit!" I laughed, "Do I have a choice? Let's get it over with."

"Okay; on three," she said. My eyes opened wide, and I started giggling. It felt like the final fucking play of an *NFL Superbowl*, and *Meg Ryan* was on top of me calling for the rock. She was half the size of me, and it crossed my mind that she may not even be strong enough for this. She was a sweetheart though, and it was a humorous moment.

"One, Two, Three!" she pulled the tubes and wires out in one hard and long motion. I moaned loudly and writhed in pain. I didn't give a shit who heard me. It hurt like a son-of-a-bitch and I felt the wires rip away from the flesh inside me. It felt like a cannonball had shot me in the stomach. I didn't realize how deep those tubes were actually in me. I lay there sweaty and wincing with my back arched and head back; sighing and laughing maniacally. Tiny drops of blood oozed from two holes in my stomach. It was by far the most painful thing I had endured yet.

Nicole was becoming tired. She stayed with me the entire time I was at the hospital. I think she only went home once to shower toward the end of my stay. Every time I woke up she would be there sitting and just being her warm, supportive self. The only reason I slept is because she was there beside me. I knew she would look out for me and make sure no one jerked me around. We were partners that had been through more challenges in seven years of marriage than some people encounter in a lifetime. This was just one more obstacle, and we knew we could beat it together. When my mom wasn't with the kids, she would also be sitting there with Nicole. They were good friends and seemed to enjoy the time together even if it was under bad circumstances. When Nicole and I were alone, we talked, but mostly we just sat and held hands. I wanted to go home, but the doctor wouldn't let me go until my bloods were stabilized, I had a bowel movement, and was walking around comfortably. My head was a mess. I couldn't think straight. I wasn't sure if it was from the low blood levels, or if it was *pumphead*. *Pumphead* is a temporary condition that patients sometimes experience as a result of being on the heart-lung bypass machine for an extended time. It left you feeling clouded mentally and not able to think straight. I was exhausted, and lethargic.

After a couple of days a physical therapist came to see me to get me up and moving. She was young and fresh out of school and has a bubbly personality. She annoyed me because she was pushy, but it was for my own good. I wanted nothing to do with getting out of bed. I wanted to just lay there until I was back to normal. She managed to get me up to walk the halls, and after a couple of times I liked it. I was challenged to walk farther each time, and I knew that if I kept at it I would get out of there quicker. One time we were walking down the hall and we passed by the CCU waiting room on the floor. A young woman was weeping as if her whole world had come crashing down. She was down on one knee holding the chair, sobbing in public. Nicole later found out that she was at the hospital because her youngest was in surgery getting an aortic aneurysm corrected and her teenage son had died only two weeks prior from a dissected aortic aneurysm. It was another sobering moment.

By around the third day Dr. Stewart was already talking about sending me home. He was arrogantly confident in my ability to recover. I guessed he was like that on account of all the cases he had seen worse than mine, and because I was so young. I was scared though. I didn't want to leave and drop dead at home from complications. Later that day a decision was made by Dr. Stewart and my medical team that I would go home on the morning of day six. I continued to spend the next few days on cloud nine, trying to collect myself mentally and gain strength. Taking a crap for the first time was a joke. After the nurse had told me that passing the first bomb was a prerequisite for my discharge, Nicole and my mom were on my case every day about it. I couldn't go six hours without one of them asking me if I had taken a shit! If they went for coffee and came back they asked if I took a shit. If they went to get a bite to eat when they came back it was "Did you take a shit?" Between the morphine and the Percocet I began to feel like every visitor who came through the door was going to ask, "Did you take a shit?" I felt like I should start asking all of them if they took a shit! Finally one afternoon I was able to squeeze one out while Nicole and my mom sat in my room waiting (probably tapping their fingers, and looking at their wristwatches). My sternum had been ripped open and the bones wired back together, and I had holes where the chest tubes were in, so imposing any kind of pressure on my stomach was impossible. I just didn't have the muscular strength, and feared that if I pushed I would rip something back open. I laughed as I sat there on the bowl. The only equivalent I could think of was an opera singer trying to hit a high note while not using their diaphragm.

The days were chock full of visits from doctors and nurses making rounds, and the nights were quiet. On the rare occasion that I was alone I found myself reflecting on the past thirty-seven years of my life. The surgery had opened up a floodgate of memories and caused me to ponder the meaning of life, and my own destiny. Nicole went home on my last day in the hospital so that she could get a good night's sleep, rejuvenate, and then come back with my mom to pick me up the next day.

On the day of my departure Dr. Stewart came by and gave me a final exam and a big hug. That part of him; the human part, separated him from the others. Good surgeons were out there, but good ones with a sense of humor, compassion, confidence, and an ability to connect with their patients were rare. He pulled my gown down in the front. "You see that?" he said, smiling and pointing to my scar. "I cut you below the shirt line." It was the first time I had seen the scar. I was amazed at how tiny it was. It was only a couple of inches long and as he said, was very low.

"Wow, pretty good!" I said, "Pretty good!" I was so happy. I had seen some real ugly heart surgery scars and others that were barely noticeable after a couple years. For the type of surgery I had, I expected my scar to be pretty big. I had seen pictures online of patients with scars that stretched from just below their collarbone to the bottom of their ribs. My brother's scar is thick and painful and has formed a *keloid* as a result of having five surgeries. He also had his first surgery at nine months old and technology was much different back then. I was hoping mine wouldn't be that bad, and I was ecstatic to see that it wasn't. I was extremely grateful to Dr. Stewart. He knew my concerns, quelled my fears, and pushed me to be strong. He left, and we spent the last few minutes in the room waiting for someone to come transport me in a wheelchair. My mom and Nicole made small talk, and I could tell they were nervous about bringing me home. They weren't nearly as nervous as I was. There was a constant buzz at the Carey house on any given day of the week and I was afraid that I wouldn't be able to hold up to a normal day at home. I hated the fact that I was so frail and weak after the surgery.

A man arrived with a wheelchair smiling and eager to help me in and bring me downstairs. He is African American and is a big man with a charisma just the same. He hummed as he put the footrests down on the wheelchair and adjusted it for me, commenting on how tall I was. I wondered what they slipped into the water at this hospital for all the employees to be so happy all the time. This guy spent his entire day wheeling people around, yet he was so friendly and concerned. I climbed into the wheelchair and said my goodbyes on the way out to all of the wonderful nurses. I was still in a foggy stupor. I sat like a zombie as they wheeled me out. The man pushing me said hello to colleagues and strangers along the way. I was still as white as a ghost from the lack of blood. Nicole and my mom walked alongside me as we made our way into the elevator. I felt like an invalid sitting there in the wheelchair in the elevator surrounded by people looking down on me. I was young, athletic, vain, and strong. It was a difficult predicament for me to be in, and it was humbling. The elevator door opened and we made our way out into the bustling main lobby. The man pushed me to the exit where we waited for the valet to bring the truck. I saw our big black SUV with the tinted windows pull up and Nicole and my mom looked at me and said, "Here we go." I was wheeled to the truck and I climbed pathetically into the back seat. Nicole and my mom got in the front and we drove away.

"Can you put the heat on?" I asked. "I'm freezing." I was cold for days after the surgery. As we merged onto the West Side Highway and began our trip to Long Island I watched the city grow smaller out the passenger window. I felt like a corpse. I never realized low blood counts could make you feel so horrible. I just sat quiet the whole ride home, responding to any questions from my mom or Nicole with short robotic answers. I didn't want to be fucked with anymore by doctors, nurses, or anyone else. I just wanted to sit and zone out.

When we arrived home they helped me out of the truck and up the porch steps. The front door swung open and my two cubs were at my legs with a much needed warm welcome. "Daddy!" they screamed.

"Hi guys! I missed you so much! It's so good to be home," I said in an animated voice. I sat down at the kitchen table and the kids proceeded to tell me a week's worth of stories at the same time, in a matter of five minutes. Nicole and my mom had set up the Montauk room (our beach themed guest room) for me so that I wouldn't have to go up and down the stairs to the master bedroom. The Montauk room was right off the kitchen and near the bathroom, which would be convenient during my recovery. We had designed the room as a result of our fondness for the ocean. It had a nautical theme with earth colored walls and was decorated with beach photos spanning two generations. The plush featherbed and overstuffed pillows were a much needed antidote for my weakened soul. I immediately went in to lie down and rest, and spent most of the first few days at home that way. On the occasions that I came out of the room, I always came carrying the cough bear they gave me at the hospital and a heavy blanket draped over my shoulders. Wherever I went the blanket and my cough bear went. The cough bear was a stuffed animal with a flat backside that the nurses told me to hold against my chest to counteract the pressure generated by the coughs on my healing sternum. I had gotten accustomed to carrying the pathetic bear everywhere, even when I didn't need it. Nicole made fun of me.

"Awe, you got your bear?" she would ask. I would smile and walk away like a weakling shaking my head. I knew I was in pathetic condition. I spent my time back and forth between the bed and the chair near the fireplace in our great room. During this time, our friends and neighbors were amazing. I was very fond of our social circle. They were classy people with good morals and family values, and during my recovery they were there for us in many ways.

Abe Lincoln once said; *And in the end, it's not the years in your life that count. It's the life in your years.*

On the first night I was home our friend Danielle knocked on the door and came to give her regards and say hi. She was the friend who had dropped us off at the hospital on the morning of my surgery. Danielle is a bubbly diva with brown wavy hair and long eyelashes. She's always fashionable and exudes a compassionate attitude to everyone she comes in contact with. Our families had moved onto the block at the same time and we were good friends. She brought dinner with her and gave us a schedule of meals that were going to be dropped off by a different friend every night for ten consecutive nights. Nicole and I were floored. The next evening, and every night after that, huge home cooked meals were dropped off by our friends. Besides being delicious, the dishes went so far as to include things that were rich in iron and would help get my blood levels back to normal. The food was incredible, and it was great to see our friends every time a meal was dropped off. I tried to feel better, but it was an extremely slow process. I was in pain, but nothing excruciating. Sometimes I would take a Percocet, but I don't like taking meds so I tried not to unless I really needed it. Overall I'm sure I took a lot less for pain after leaving the hospital than most patients. My head continued to feel like mush from the low bloods. A couple of days after I had gotten home I had an appointment with my cardiologist Dr. Walsh. It was a bad day for me and I felt incoherent. I just sat there in a chair in the treatment room feeling dazed and confused during the visit. Months later my cardiologist and the staff there would tell me how bad I looked. Nicole later told me that during that visit I didn't remember where I worked, and had a hard time answering simple questions.

Later that day, the office called Nicole with the results of my blood tests. They told her that my *hemoglobin* and red blood counts were still low and that I would have to come back and have blood drawn every single day until my levels returned to normal. I moped around with my cape on trying to stay warm. I felt like Superman after his encounter with *Kryptonite*. There was so much I wanted to do, but I didn't have the energy or mental capacity. All I did was pace around the house, sleep, or sit in the chair near the fireplace and stare out the wall of windows in the great room. Life went on outside, but mine seemed to pause. I didn't feel like I was getting any better.

One morning toward the end of the second week I woke up to take a piss and could barely stand up to finish. My knees got weak, and I felt a significant weakness and uneasiness in my stomach. *Fuck. This is not good,* I thought. I heard Nicole in the kitchen taking dishes out of the dishwasher and putting them away. The kids had already left for school. I came out and sat at the kitchen table and hung my head. "What's the matter?" She asked.

"I feel like shit."

"What do you mean?"

"I can't explain it; I just don't feel good, something isn't right. Just leave me alone for a minute"

"I'm going to take your blood pressure and heart rate," said Nicole. We had borrowed an electronic blood pressure/heart-rate machine from our neighbors across the street. Bob and Kris Tallman were a little older than us, and had taken us under their wing when we moved into the neighborhood. They were always there for us, and Bob was the resident expert on the block on many topics and widely consulted. He always had time for me, and I appreciated the guidance over the years.

She put the cuff on me and started the machine. It finished inflating and beeped. "I need to call the doctor," she said as it finished.

"Why, what are the readings?"

"Your blood pressure is low and your heart rate is high," she said.

"Oh man," I sighed. *Am I going to die?* I thought. *I make it through the brutal surgery and now I'm going to fucking keel over in my house in front of my family? This is just great!*

Nicole got my cardiologist Dr. Walsh on the phone and I could hear her becoming agitated. He wouldn't see me because he felt I needed more serious attention and Nicole was annoyed. She wanted to get me somewhere as soon as possible and Dr. Walsh was local, but he obviously knew what was about to transpire and he recommended she take me to the hospital. Nicole refused to take me to the E.R. and called Dr. Stewart on his cell phone. He told her to bring me in immediately and they would take care of me. After some quick phone calls to arrange care for the kids; we were in the truck and on the way back to *New York-Presbyterian.* I couldn't believe it. I sat in the back seat feeling like an idiot. I felt like a used car that was constantly in repair. I was angry, and more afraid than on my first trip to the hospital for surgery. They had tinkered around with the organ that kept me alive; stopping it, leaving me dead for a few hours, cutting off hoses and reconnecting them, and then jumpstarting it back into submission. I felt that there were so many complexities to the procedure that it could be any number of things gone wrong. We arrived at the Millstein building, gave the car to the valet, and made our way up to Dr. Stewart's office. Nicole checked me in and we sat in the same familiar office where I had seen *Dr. Oz* pass by a month ago. Moments later Dr. Stewart's colleague Tracey Andrews came out wearing a white lab coat and carrying a clipboard. She has short blonde hair and like the rest of the staff at *New York-Presbyterian,* she is friendly and very knowledgeable. She led us back to a treatment room which was very small with an exam table and some tools. When we got inside the cramped room, Nicole and I explained the whole story, and she took my vitals.

"I bet my heart rate is up to 150," I said. My heart was racing, and I couldn't control it. It was the worst feeling and I felt helpless.

"153 beats per minute," she said as she let go of my wrist. Nicole was panicking. I just shook my head.

What the fuck, I thought, *this is ridiculous.* I remembered my friend who had a similar surgery telling me that sometimes after open heart surgery the heart would go into an irregular beating pattern. He had to make a return trip back to the hospital a few days after being home to get his heart jumpstarted back into a normal rhythm. I sat there as my heart beat out of my chest. My heart rate was through the roof as if I was in the middle of a run, and I couldn't do anything to lower it.

"What is this from? What do we do?" asked Nicole.

"This is not uncommon after surgery, his heart rhythm is off. He is in what is referred to as atrial flutter," Tracey said. He needs medical attention, so we are going to admit him. We are going to administer some meds to try and regulate his heart rhythm, and monitor him." The door opened and Dr. Stewart appeared.

"So it looks like you will be staying until we can get this straightened out." He handed me some pills to take with a cup of water. "We've called down to the cardiac unit, and as soon as a bed is ready they will let us know."

"Great," I said miserably.

"Don't be so glum. We'll get this straightened out."

"I'm not going to have to get shocked am I?" I asked. That was my worst fear; as bad as my fear of the surgery itself. I did not want to be paddled like those poor bastards I saw them do it to on television.

"No," he said. "We should be able to regulate this with medicine." And with that he nodded and smiled at Nicole. He put his hand on my shoulder, squeezed me, and the all-star left the room.

"Okay, it's probably going to be a few minutes, so try and stay comfortable and I'll be back as soon as we can get you down there," said Tracey.

She left the room and Nicole and I looked at each other. I shook my head and she just stared at me. We both knew this was not going to be a pleasant visit. We were both starving and had not eaten since we left the house that morning. I felt even worse because Nicole was five months pregnant. She was being stubborn and wouldn't go down to the cafe until I was settled in a bed. We remained in that miserable room for over two and a half hours. Debbie, Dr. Stewart's office manager brought Nicole a snack. Finally a nurse came with a wheelchair to bring me down to the cardiac unit.

I had a team of a dozen various doctors come by and examine me in the first hour. Something was wrong and they didn't have an immediate resolution for it. Nicole became frustrated with the number of unfamiliar faces visiting me and checking me out. She began to interrogate every person who crossed the line into my room. Within two minutes she knew their name, title, education, and how much they knew about me. She was characteristically thorough. I just sat there in the bed like a broken fool while she handled everything. Life felt fragile and uncertain, and for the first time I found myself at a tipping point beyond anyone's control; not sure if I would prevail or fall into the darkness. In the hours that followed Nicole and I continued to watch my erratic blood pressure and heartbeat. The doctors continued to come by, yet there were no solutions. I did not see much of Dr. Stewart because he was the surgeon, and this issue was better suited to the cardiologists and electrologists. Nicole did however confirm that he was kept abreast of everything and no decisions were made without his consultation.

It was 3:00 a.m., and I sat in the dark listening to the beep of the monitor. Nicole was asleep in the chair next to me. She had to have been exhausted. She had held my hand and cried earlier in the evening because the doctors could not get my heart rate under control. They had also given us some bad news that I had fluid around my heart. I was shitting bricks about having to be opened up again. I had heard of people having to be reopened because of complications and they were miserable situations. My veins were flat, and because of that one of the nurses had brutalized a vein on an insertion attempt. I had a quarter size black and blue on the top of my hand that was killing me. I iced it, but it was extremely painful. They were finally able to get two I.V.'s in me. I felt completely burned out. I stared out the window at the city lights, and wondered if I was going to make it out of the hospital in time for Thanksgiving, only days away. Then I wondered if I would make it out at all. This wasn't a little angina; the main organ that kept me alive was hacked open and cut up two weeks ago, and now it wasn't working properly. I wasn't sure if death was right around the corner. I was depressed and missed my kids. My whole family had been through the ringer. My parents had gone back upstate and my mom was very upset about me having to go back into the hospital. She did not like being so far away. She promised to come down with my sister and the rest of my family and prepare a Thanksgiving feast.

By morning my vital signs had not changed. Nicole was starting to get belligerent about the fact that they had not yet figured out what to do for me. We were told that the head cardiologist was going to be meeting with us that morning. We had it with the lack of answers and uncertainties. When the doctor arrived she told us that the medicine was not working. Nicole and I both got restless. "You are going to have to be cardioverted," she said. I had never heard that term before, but I knew what it meant. I was going to have to be shocked! I was going to have to be zapped with electricity in order to straighten out my misbehaving heart.

"You're kidding right?" I said to the doctor.

"No Mr. Carey, your heart is not in normal sinus rhythm. This has to be done."

"So when are you going to do this?"

"Well, we need to make sure there are no clots in your heart before we cardiovert you so we are going to have to do a tee echo first."

"Oh my God," I sighed. I put my head down and cried silently. I was tired and overwhelmed. They were going to have to put a probe down my esophagus while I was awake; all the way down near my heart to check for clots. Then after this torture they were going to blast me with a few hundred volts of electricity to attempt to reset my heart rhythm. Through all of this I would be awake, which is what terrified me most. They put you in a sort of "half-sleep" for all of this. They didn't knock you out completely, and in my opinion that was the worst part about it. It's one thing to sleep through it all, but the fact that I was going to be remotely conscious changed everything. I zoned out for a moment. Flashes of my children ran through my mind. I saw my five year old Milan running on the playground with her long sandy-blonde locks blowing in the air, an image of my wedding day, flashbacks of my childhood, and then an image of my two year old Preston laughing like a maniac on a swing.

"Mr. Carey are you okay?" The doctor touched my shoulder.

I looked over at her. "Yeah, I'm okay. I just can't believe this. This is worse than the surgery. I thought the surgery was going to be unbearable, and it's been all the other stuff that has taken its toll on me."

"Well, we are going to get you back on track."

"What if it doesn't work?"

"Let's stay positive okay? Can you do that?" asked the doctor.

I looked over at Nicole. Tears had streamed her cheeks. I turned to the doctor, "Yeah, I don't have a choice."

"Okay," said the doctor, "we are going to do the tee echo at 11:00 a.m. You will be given twilight anesthesia, meaning you will be half awake and half asleep. This is necessary because you need to be awake enough swallow the probe as it is inserted. Once we confirm there are no clots on your heart the electrologist will cardiovert you. We have to ensure there are no blood clots behind your heart before you are cardioverted otherwise the shock could jostle them loose causing them to enter your blood stream, potentially leading to a stroke."

"Okay," I said. At this point there were no more questions. I had surrendered to the fact that they were going to do whatever they thought was necessary to keep me alive, and I didn't have a choice in the matter. Who knew how brutal it was going to get? I prepared myself mentally for whatever God was going to deal me. What was the point in asking any more questions or delaying it any longer? I surrendered. I was walking closer to the other side than I ever thought I would be at thirty-seven years old. I have never been more afraid in my life. When the doctor left Nicole made calls to family to give them updates. She was exhausted, and rightly so. I could tell by her mannerisms and behavior that she too was unsure about whether I was going to make it out of the hospital. She rubbed my forehead and stroked my hair. It felt like she was preparing to say goodbye. "Are you okay?" she asked.

"I'm fine," I said in a frustrated manner. "I just want to get this fucking shit over with and go home. If I don't get home for Thanksgiving I'm going to be pissed off. I can't believe this. I can't believe this is actually happening. Everything goes fine with the open heart surgery, and now my body decides to pussy out? First it's the issue with the blood; the low *hemoglobin* and *hematocrit*, and the transfusion. Now it's a fucked up heart rate and blood pressure, and fluid on my heart. I've never been this fucking weak in my life!" I went on a ten minute rant, and Nicole just listened, which is exactly what I needed. She didn't disagree, tell me to be positive, or ask me to stop. She just sat and listened.

A moment later, one of the nurses came in. "Mrs. Carey, I thought you might want this." It was a tray of hot food. Nicole looked surprised. "You need to take care of yourself and that baby too," said the nurse.

"Thank you that was very kind," she said, sitting up in her chair. The nurse put the tray down on the table next to her and rubbed her back for a moment.

"If you guys need anything else, just let us know." She walked out of the room and we both looked at each other. We were not only surprised, but moved by how caring the nurses were. There were many interactions like that, where we felt it in our hearts that these people really cared about us. They made us feel like we were in this together, and it was a good feeling. Nicole was very hungry, and I felt guilty as I watched her woof down the roast beef and mashed potatoes on the tray. It was a moment that kind of amplified how badly things had spun out of control in the past few days. My poor pregnant wife was starving herself sitting at my bedside, probably afraid to leave because she might find me dead when she came back.

At 11:15 a.m. two big carts with machines on them were pushed into my room and the teams for the tee echo and cardioversion arrived at my bedside. The anesthesiologist explained everything he was going to do, and how the whole ordeal was going to go down. I kissed Nicole and they drew the curtain to my bedside closed. They wouldn't allow her to be by my bedside during the procedure so she stood outside the curtain and waited. The anesthesiologist administered the first dose of drugs and I began to feel high. I wasn't tired, I just felt drunk. She asked me to turn on my side and raise my arms above my head. She kept talking to me and let me know that they would be inserting the probe in a moment. I lay there with my eyes closed, but not asleep. I felt high as a kite; halfway between dreamland and consciousness. "Okay Mr. Carey, you are going to open your mouth and swallow as we insert the probe. You are going to keep swallowing until I tell you to stop."

"Okay," I mumbled in an inebriated state. She inserted what felt like a piece of cord from a fucking weedwacker into my throat. I swallowed on command until I was told to rest. I don't remember too much after that. My next memory was waking up crying. I couldn't see anything as I was still in a drunken state with my eyes closed. I heard the doctor's voice; "It's over. You did well."

"Did the cardioversion work? Did it fix my heartbeat?" I asked.

"Yes, it worked. And your aorta repair looks gorgeous."

I cried and laughed hysterically at the same time. I had lost complete control of my emotions because of the anesthesia. "I love you," I told the doctor. "I love you guys, you are the best! Thank you so much!" I told them. I felt as if I were just handed back my life; given a pass to keep going. I felt Nicole's lips press on my forehead, and I fell asleep. I woke up at 2:00 a.m. to the familiar beep-beep of the monitors. It was dark in the room, and the bright light from the nurses' station in the hallway dimly lit the room I was in. I turned to the window where the city lights glistened like diamonds dropped on blacktop. I took a deep breath and was glad to be alive. Nicole was curled up in a chair next to me sleeping. She was my soldier; a woman who would do anything for me, and I for her. This experience would be another stripe on our pockets. I sat and watched her sleep in the chair and it dawned on me that there are people in the world who would never get to experience what it feels like to have a relationship like this. I felt grateful to be with her; to have met her and put this great life together. It was the first time since I went in for surgery that I felt inspired.

In the morning exams revealed that my heart rate was much better, but still not where it needed to be. It was finally in normal sinus rhythm, but needed to come down to a reasonable rate. Nicole was uneasy all day and wouldn't rest until things improved significantly. By that evening my heart rate and blood pressure were stabilized, but I was coughing and the doctors started talking of the fluid around my heart. *Pericardial effusion* as they called it was not a condition to be taken lightly. They put me on a couple of different medicines, one of which was called *Colchizene* to reduce the fluid. I was particularly frightened because I heard *Bill Clinton* had developed this condition after surgery and they had to go in and drain the fluid. I was not having that. I had been through enough, so I focused mentally on willing the fluid out. The next couple of days were tough on me. I sent Nicole home to get a hot shower, see the kids, and take care of herself. Being that she was pregnant, I was concerned for her safety. There were only a few days left until Thanksgiving, and I was getting nervous about not being home for the holiday. That would crush my spirit. After being stabilized they moved me to a low level unit, and there wasn't much happening there. In ICU, and CCU, the lights were bright and there was always some sort of buzz going on. My new room was quiet, and although the nurses were phenomenal; they did not come to check on me as often. I lay in bed feeling lonely; wondering what was going to happen next. Was the worst behind me or was I going to have to get opened up again so they could drain the fluid around my heart? I refused to give in to the problem and I stayed positive. Two days later I had a CT scan done to determine the significance of the condition. My nurse confirmed there was some fluid around my heart, but told me that I would have to wait and speak with the doctor for official results. Later that evening I lay in bed watching television. I didn't have the capacity for anything that required mental energy, and I was lonely so I kept it on for background noise. I fell in and out of sleep throughout the night.

In the morning Dr. Stewart and Tracey appeared at the foot of my bed. "What are you doing?" he asked. "Get dressed you're going home!"

"Really!" I asked.

"Yes, get ready you're going home today. Call your wife."

"What about the pericardial effusion?"

"I read your CT scan. It's not significant enough for me to worry about it or be concerned."

"Oh awesome! Thank you so much Dr. Stewart. This past week has been a rollercoaster."

"Well, you're going home now. You're going to be fine. You'll see your cardiologist on Monday after Thanksgiving. You are going to continue to take the *Colchizene*, and a diuretic for a short time to address any residual fluid, and you're going to stay on the blood thinners until we feel you are not at risk for any further heart beat irregularities. This is to prevent clots so that if God forbid there is another issue, you will be able to be cardioverted without having to be subjected to another tee echo. I am also doubling your dosage of *Toperol* to help your heart beat stay regular, and keeping you on iron until your *hemoglobin* and *hematocrit* are back up to normal."

"Whatever, I'm just happy to be going home!"

"Okay, get dressed and gather your things. There's no rush. When Nicole get's here ring for the nurse and she will get you checked out. I'll see you in six weeks."

"Great, thanks again Dr. Stewart, and have a happy Thanksgiving!" I called Nicole the moment that they left. "I'm coming home!" I said.

"Really!"

"Yes, Dr. Stewart just left"

"What about the pericardial effusion?"

"He read the CT scan from yesterday and said it was nothing to be concerned about."

"Oh, that's great news. I'm so happy. My mom should be here shortly and I will come right in and get you."

"Okay, I love you, I'll see you soon. Give the kids a kiss and tell them *Big Strong Bear* is coming home."

"'Kay, love you. See you soon."

A couple of hours later Nicole arrived. I walked out of the hospital slowly this time. No wheelchair. I was angry at my body and ready to battle back into condition. The valet pulled up the truck and a gentleman opened the heavy glass door for us to exit the hospital. It was rainy and cold outside, and I crawled into the back seat. I mumbled a few words to Nicole on the way home, but I was mostly in and out of sleep. We made a stop at the pharmacy to get the dozen medications I was prescribed. Our friend Michelle was the pharmacist and she peeked her head out to say hi when Nicole came out with the medications.

As we turned onto our block I told myself that I was not going back to the hospital again. We pulled into the driveway and as I got out of the truck, the cold wet air stung my face. As we made our way up the path to the house, the kids struggled to open the heavy mahogany door. They were elbowing each other for room to see who could get out first. My five year old Milan yelled "Hi daddy!" as my two year old boy Preston squeezed under her arm and ran out the front door with no coat or shoes on. No matter how many times we yelled at him he would always go outside without socks and shoes. He bolted down the porch steps and onto the cold wet bricks; barefoot in November. He hugged my leg and said "Oh daddy, I love you." It was an emotional moment, and a voice inside me was thanking God. That image of him running down the porch steps and grabbing on to my leg in the rain will forever be embedded in my mind. It was a turning point in my life. It was like a scene from an *Oliver Stone* movie as we stood there; him hugging my leg, and me struggling to reach down and put my arms around him; both of us oblivious to the cold rain pouring down on us. I thanked God to be alive to touch him. My son and I are very close, and it was a pivotal moment in my recovery where I gained strength and motivation to get well, and push myself to the next level.

I had been through a lot of challenges in my life. I had a childhood that most people couldn't fathom, and I had grown into a full blown alcoholic, criminal and degenerate by the age of eighteen. On November 16, 1990 at the age of eighteen I went into alcohol and drug rehab for the second time and I finally got sober. From that point on I had put together a beautiful life in spite of having little resources or tools to do so. I did it with a strong will, and an unwavering fight against the odds.

I knew after my second trip to the hospital that I couldn't resort to a state of depression. I realized that I would be fine if I started addressing my recovery from open heart surgery the same way I had all of the other challenges in my life. There are hundreds of people that have open heart surgery everyday and survive, but that wasn't good enough for me. I wanted to resume the path I was on before I had surgery.

Thanksgiving was relaxed and intimate. My parents and siblings came down. We spent a lot of time lounging around the fireplace being lazy and chatting quietly. It was exactly what I needed after the five days of torture I had just gone through in the hospital. The days and weeks that followed were tough. I didn't want to do anything social or be around anyone except my family. I avoided anything that required mental or emotional energy, and I didn't touch a computer, handle any business, or return telephone calls. I was drained and it was time for me and my family to heal. I was happy to be able to have dinner with them, tuck my children into their beds every night, and see them in the morning before they went to school. Normally I would be on the train during those times.

Christmas decorating was interesting. Instead of climbing a ladder to hang lights outside like I normally would, I sat in a chair on the porch with a heavy jacket on directing Nicole how to do everything. I had kept in touch with my biological father who I had rekindled a relationship with a few months earlier. In December, he and his wife Nancy came from Florida to visit us in Long Island. The only way I was able to move forward was to convince myself that he wasn't the person that he was when I was a child. They spent about four days, and it turned out to be a nice visit. It softened the baggage I carried from my childhood and served as a starting point for our new relationship.

A couple weeks later we spent a quiet Christmas at home, and declined all of the New Year's parties we were invited to. I still didn't have the energy or confidence to do much. In January I started Cardiac Rehab at the St. Francis DeMatteis center. My surgeon Dr. Stewart said that formal cardiac rehab wasn't necessary for me, but I elected to do it because I planned on testing my body and working out hard. I wanted the supervision in a center where doctors were present should anything happen to me. Dr. Walsh my cardiologist cleared me to start and I made the appointment for my first session.

Nicole and I arrived at the Dematteis Center at 8:00 a.m. I had heard great things about the place and was excited to start rehab. It was bitter cold, and we rushed up the long winding path to the entrance. Huge automatic glass doors whooshed open and we entered onto the richly polished marble floors of the lobby. A security guard pointed us in the direction of the cardiac rehab center, and we chuckled at the ebony grand piano playing by itself as we walked by. Oil paintings of donors and philanthropists hung on the walls in the hallway. As we entered the rehab center Nicole went to the reception desk and immediately began the check-in, completing the paperwork necessary for my intake. I bypassed her and headed over to a doorway to catch a glimpse of the main exercise floor. Immediately I felt awkward and uncomfortable. Everyone there was significantly older than me, and I felt like I stuck out like a sore thumb. There was an indoor track that went around the perimeter of the floor and exercise equipment on each side of it. There were also medical stations on each side of the track; one where people were handing in what looked like exercise cards, and another where people were having heart monitors put on. My eyes turned to the people walking briskly around the track; old people. I turned my head to the treadmills; old people. I turned quickly to the stairmasters, exercise bikes, and to the people stretching on the mat; all old people! All I could think at the moment was "*Cocoon!*" It was like the movie *Cocoon*, and I had to be at least ten years younger than anyone there. I was by no means prejudiced; just very uncomfortable. I shook my head and decided I was going through with it anyway. I walked back to Nicole who was sitting in a chair filling out my paperwork on a clipboard. She looked up.

"What's the problem?" she asked.

"Nothing," I laughed. "It's just weird because everyone is so old. I don't give a shit, I'm still doing it. I don't want to keel over at the gym."

"Oh my God," she said, "you're something!"

On that first visit I was given a fitness assessment by a nurse, met with the head cardiologist of the program, and I sat through sessions on nutrition, and open heart surgery recovery. At the end of the visit they told me to return on Monday to start a three day a week program. I left excited to start exercising again.

"Will you come back with me on Monday?" I asked Nicole as we were walking to the truck.

"If you want me to."

"Yeah, it would be nice if you came to the first couple of sessions," I said.

My doctors told me that the exercise sessions would leave me feeling exhausted, so my plan was to work at my home office on the days that I wasn't going to rehab, and transition back to headquarters as I regained my strength. As with everything else the guys at the office told me to take as much time as I needed. They were great throughout the whole ordeal.

Rehab at the Demmateis center was terrific. I had a fear of being alone in the gym and dropping dead of over exertion, so being under medical supervision during my workouts gave me tremendous comfort. I needed to get some good workouts under my belt and test the new heart before I felt comfortable enough to go off on my own. The other patients ranged from heart attack victims to a patient with an LVAD (Left Ventricular Assist Device). The man with the LVAD scared me. An LVAD is a machine for people in the end stages of heart failure. It does the work of a heart. I couldn't imagine depending on a little electronic pump to keep you alive. It was impressive but frightening to me. My early workouts were a joke. I thought I was going to quit because they were so easy. They weren't even working me hard enough to break a sweat. After a couple of days one of the physiologists pulled me to the side with my chart. She was about my age, wore green scrubs, and had a whistle around her neck. She seemed to be more in tuned to the progression of my workouts than the rest of the staff.

"Mr. Carey, I adjusted your workouts. I know you are getting bored, and I don't want you to leave," she said. I smiled at her.

"Thank You," I said. "I really appreciate that."

Over the next month I gradually worked myself up to a sweat producing workout. I was nervous that at any time something might blow or come loose in my chest, but I felt comfort in knowing that the doctors and nurses were watching me on the EKG monitor during the workouts. In February I began traveling to the Hoboken office a few days a week, and going to rehab on the alternate days. It was a difficult transitory period when I was beginning to resume my previous workloads in both business and personal matters, but was not one-hundred percent recovered. I was constantly exhausted, and sometimes felt as if I were going to pass out on my feet. I became agitated with the perception that I was healed. People didn't realize how draining a typical day was for me. I was constantly nervous about blowing a hose rushing back and forth to the train. People were generally supportive with my recovery; most were amazing. I found it humorous though how some could be so out of touch with what I had been through. Some people never called or even reached out to say "hey I'm thinking of you." It was hard to grasp, because I knew if the tables were turned, I would have been there for them at all costs. Rather than get resentful though, I pitied them. They were the type of people who would end up old with no real substance in their lives.

By March I was back full steam. I put in a lot of hours at the office to try and catch up. We had been brutalized financially due to a number of events that happened, but especially as a result of the surgery and both of us being out of work. I was miserable commuting four hours a day to work and I was burning the candle at both ends to make up ground because I knew I would have to be out again when Nicole had the baby in April. She was doing great, but her checkups had become a rollercoaster because the baby kept flip flopping between breached and normal. We were both nervous because she had my previous two children naturally, and now there was a remote possibility of her having to have a cesarean section if the baby were breached in the ninth month. It was something Nicole wanted no part of. Like me, she was active, vain, and frightened of having to go under the knife. I was against a C-section because I didn't want her to have to sacrifice her body for the child, nor have to endure what I expected to be a rough recovery as compared to natural childbirth. On her last checkup before delivery the baby was head down. We were both excited and her *OB* scheduled her for induction on April 14th.

We had chosen to have the baby at *Lenox Hill* hospital in Manhattan where we had our other two children. Some of our family and friends couldn't understand why we were driving all the way back into Manhattan to have the baby, but that's because they didn't have the experiences we did. We had become very close with Nicole's *OB/GYN* Dr. Lisa Johnson. She had delivered our previous two children and was one of those rare doctors who has esteemed credentials combined with a genuinely nurturing way. *Lenox Hill* was consistently one of the top ranked maternity programs in the country, and we had gotten to know the doctors and nurses there pretty well. We couldn't see having the baby anywhere else. It was a difficult time for us to be having a baby, but the event became a breath of fresh air after having been through so much in the previous six months.

We arrived on the 14th at the crack of dawn, and my plan was to get Nicole settled, make an appearance at my office to wrap up some business, and then return to the hospital to be there for the final hours and delivery. In the past I had been at her bedside for every second, but unfortunately I had missed so much time in the office because of my surgery that I had to prioritize what days I would take off. I had agreed with the guys at the office to be around right up until birth and then to be out for three or four days afterward. I was not happy about it, as I had taken two full weeks off when each of my previous children were born, but circumstances were different and I was in no position to be out again. Nicole and I parked and then ate breakfast at our favorite diner near the hospital. It was nice to have some alone time with her. We kept the conversation light, held hands across the table, and joked about the passersby. When we were finished we walked down the block to the hospital.

Lenox Hill is known for having a great maternity ward. It isn't the fanciest, or ritziest of all the hospitals in the city, but it has a feeling and culture associated with it that makes it very popular. It is the hospital of "New Yorkers", and also the hospital of choice for many celebrities; most notably *Sarah Jessica Parker*. Dr. Johnson is highly respected in the maternity ward and had given the staff a heads up that we were coming in to deliver number three. When we checked in the intake staff was very friendly as usual. It was comforting to see so many familiar smiles, and reunite with some of the doctors and nurses we had gotten to know over the years. It was so much nicer than having a delivery surrounded by strangers. Within an hour they had Nicole set up in a bed in the maternity ward. They treated us very well. After I knew Nicole was settled and okay I conferred privately with the nurse and then headed to my office. I was a little nervous, but I reminded myself how long the progression took for the previous two births. It took about a half-hour to get into my office in Hoboken.

I had just gotten settled when the phone rang. "Hey, it's me," said Nicole, "you'll never believe it."

"What?" I asked. She started hysterical crying. My heart raced and anxiety caused blood to rush to my face like pins and needles.

"They just did a sonogram, and the baby is breached!" My heart stopped. I was so angry and disappointed.

"Well, it will turn," I said. We didn't know the baby's sex, because we wanted it to be a surprise so everyone still referred to it asexually.

"I don't think so; I have a bad feeling about this. I had a dream a couple of weeks ago that I had to have a C-section."

"Would you stop?" I said, "You are so negative. It's going to be fine, the baby will turn, you'll see."

"Well when are you coming here?" she asked.

"I need to finish some things here and then I'll come."

"What do you mean finish up? Are you kidding me? You were here for every second of your other two, and stayed home for two weeks afterward!"

"Nicole, what the fuck do you want me to do? I've missed so much time because of my surgery. This is not a position I want to be in, but I can't do anything about it. I'm sorry. Let me go so I can wrap some things up and I'll come right over."

"Fine," she said, and hung up.

My eyes watered, and I sat there for a moment and just stared at the computer screen shaking my head. I rubbed my forehead frustrated with the circumstances. I didn't mean to snap at her. After all, she never left my side during my hospitalization. I felt guilty. I hustled to finish up some last minute projects, and then I headed over to the hospital.

The smell of bagels and coffee filled the air as I came up out of the subway on 77th Street and Lexington Avenue. I considered the city my hometown after fourteen years of living there, and contrary to what most people think of it, it had a soothing effect on me. Nicole and I had often spoken of returning to live there in retirement. As I rode the elevator up to the maternity ward on the fifth floor I knew I was in for a long night.

When I arrived Nicole was anxious, and glad to see me. I talked her down to a more relaxed state and she filled me in on everything that was going on. "They're going to give me an epidural and then try and move the baby manually. They call it aversion," she said.

"Okay, that sounds like a plan. I'm sure it will work," I said. I was an eternal optimist. Doctor Johnson, Nicole's *OB/GYN* came in with a team of about six others. Apparently performing an *aversion* was such a rare thing at the hospital that everyone wanted to witness it. It was interesting to watch the primitive procedure. Nicole lay on her back surrounded by a horseshoe of doctors at the foot of the bed. Dr. Johnson and a colleague began to feel out the positioning of the baby in her stomach and turn it by pushing on the back of the head, and underside of the butt. It wasn't painful for Nicole, but after three or four tries they had to give up.

"Can't you keep trying?" I asked.

"No," Dr. Johnson said. "If we continue to try turning the baby unsuccessfully, it could cause distress and a rapid increase in heart rate. We don't want that." I turned my back to them and looked out the big window overlooking the city and ran my fingers through my hair.

"So now what?" I asked annoyed.

"I just want to have a C-section and get this over with," said Nicole. "I'm okay with it. I already resigned to the fact that this baby was going to be a C-section from the beginning. I felt it, I dreamt it, and I've succumbed to it. Let's do it while I am mentally prepared." The other option was for us to go back home and wait and see if the baby turned again, however Nicole had already been administered the epidermal and she wanted no part of returning in a week to start the whole thing all over again with no guarantee anyway. "Let's just do the C-section," she said. Dr. Johnson looked over at me for my reaction. She is a tall and curvy black woman with a gorgeous face and a southern warmness about her. Our previous two births with her were like fairytales. She went above and beyond what you would expect in every way, and this birth was no exception. Her visit to the hospital to see me during my own ordeal is a true testament to the kind of person she is.

"What?" I asked as she looked at me. "What do you want me to say? I don't want her to have to go through a C-section. I feel bad for her."

"Ben!" Nicole interrupted "It's going to be okay. I'll be fine. I'm having this baby today." I looked at her, and then I turned and made eye contact with Dr. Johnson.

"It will be fine honey; really," said Dr. Johnson.

With that, she and Nicole smiled at each other, nodded, and Dr. Johnson left the room. The attending started checking Nicole's vitals and I asked her, "How bad is her recovery going to be if she has a C-section?"

"Not bad," said the doctor.

"Do you think this is the right decision?" I asked.

"Yes. There's no doubt about it. It is much safer for her to have this procedure in a controlled environment, than wait past the due date, lose more fluid around the baby, and potentially go into the labor with a baby in breeched position."

"Will a plastic surgeon be doing the stitches?" I asked. The doctor laughed at me as she stood next to Nicole's bedside.

"No. Your doctor will be doing that."

"Really?" I asked. "*OB*'s do surgery too?"

"Yes, and just so you know; Dr. Johnson is the most highly regarded surgeon in the hospital, and I'm not just saying that to make you feel comfortable. She's good."

I raised my eyebrows, having been put in check. "Okay," I said. She left, and for the next hour Nicole and I chatted nervously about the kids, the house; anything to keep our minds occupied. Then Dr. Johnson arrived. She smiled and walked over to Nicole's bedside and gently brushed her forehead. "Are you ready?" she asked.

"Sure, let's go," said Nicole with a smile.

"Alright then," said Dr. Johnson looking my way. I nodded at her. "I'm going to scrub in. The nurse will bring Nicole into the operating room. Ben, you'll stay in the room and I will send a nurse when we're ready for you. Are we all clear?" She looked at us both.

"Yes," I said with a smile.

"Okay see you soon," she said and she patted Nicole's thigh and walked out. The nurse remained in the room and started disconnecting monitors and preparing Nicole to be transported. I walked over to Nicole's bedside and gave her a kiss and stroked her hair.

"Are you going to be okay?" I asked.

"Yeah, I'll be fine. I knew it was going to come to this. Like I said earlier, for some reason I just knew in my heart that this baby was going to be a C-section."

"Okay," I said. "I'm going to make some phone calls and give everyone updates, and I guess I'll see you in the room okay?"

"Okay, love you."

I walked out of the room and heard them wheeling Nicole out behind me. I went down the hall and past the double doors to the waiting room to call our parents and let everyone know what was going on. After about a half hour a male doctor; the anesthesiologist pushed open one of the double doors and yelled out to me. "Mr. Carey! There you are! What are you doing?" The man has a heavy Russian accent and I looked at him quizzically; partly entertained by the cool accent, but also not sure what the hell the problem was. When he first approached me I thought maybe my cell phone was interfering with a CT scan or something.

"What do you mean?" I asked.

He smiled. "We told you that we would get you from the room when your wife was ready. Dr. Johnson thinks you left because you couldn't take the stress!" We both started laughing and he put his arm on my shoulder and we began walking to the operating room. On the way he grabbed a set of scrubs and hit me in the chest with them. "Here put these on, and make it quick. They're ready for you."

"Okay," I said. I rushed into the bathroom and put on the scrubs as quickly as I could without ripping them. Definitely not *Grey's Anatomy* I thought, as I looked in the mirror at the cheap paper scrubs and shower cap. More like *McDoofus*. Then I turned and bolted out the door nervously. A female nurse was waiting for me and she smiled when I came out.

"Okay here we go, follow me," she said. We walked down the hallway and through the double doors into the operating room. I immediately felt dizzy and got knots in my stomach. Nicole was lying with her head toward me, and a big curtain hung, blocking the view from her shoulders down. "Hi Honey!" she said upside down.

"Hi Honey!" Dr. Johnson called out from a place I couldn't see her. I shook my head and rubbed my forehead. *Like a fucking circus trick,* I thought. *Jesus Christ.* It reminded me of that magic trick where they put a body in a box and saw it in half. The Russian doctor who summoned me from the hallway was standing nearby analyzing monitors and had a huge smile and just chuckled at me. There was a stool at the head of the table near Nicole's head and he motioned for me to sit down.

"Relax," he said. "Everything is going to be just fine Benjamin. Your wife is doing great."

"Okay," I said nervously.

"Where is the Ipod that you had?" he asked.

"Oh, I think I left it in the last room we were in."

"Well I'll have someone fetch it for you. Do you want it?"

"That would be great," I said nodding. He was a very cool guy and made me feel comfortable. He took great care of my wife, had the anesthesia on point, and was very outgoing. A few moments later a nurse appeared with my Ipod and the Russian plugged me in. *Ray Lamontagne* sang, *Baby It's been a long day, baby, Things ain't been going my way, And now I need you here, to clear my mind all the time, And baby....* He was our favorite, and *You are the Best Thing* couldn't have been a more fitting backdrop for the scene going down. I sat on the rolling stool opposite Nicole's head. I cupped her cheeks and kissed her on the forehead. "Everything is going to be fine," I told her. She laughed at me.

"Are you going to be fine?" she asked, "You're pale as a ghost."

"Whatever, I'm fine."

"Yeah okay," she said smiling at me. I sat there nervous and fidgeting. I could only imagine what was happening on the other side of the curtain. I'm sure they would have let me take a peep, but I was so disgusted with the whole idea that my eyes didn't even glance near the horizon of that curtain. I had heard that they take out all of a woman's organs and put them on her chest in order to take out the baby, and then they put them back in. Not something I needed a graphic visual on. I was an easier sell on the Immaculate Conception. In fact, I made sure that I didn't even look at anything reflective behind the curtain for fear of seeing what was taking place behind there. I hadn't been in there long at all when Dr. Johnson peeked over the curtain and said "We're almost there, are you ready to see the baby?"

"Yes!" we said in unison. Neither of us knew whether it was a boy or girl. We didn't find out with our previous two, but our guesses were the same on both and coincidentally we were right on both. This time around though, I thought it was a boy, and Nicole was convinced that it was a girl. There was going to be a showdown this time! She felt so strongly that it was a girl that I thought she may have found out on one of her checkups that she had gone to without me. That insecurity was put to rest about five minutes later when Dr. Johnson called out "Here's the baby!" I stood up and looked over the curtain and she held out a slime covered little infant with a penis.

"Holy shit!" I yelled "it's a boy! It's a God damn boy! I can't believe it! Oh my God, it's a boy! I told you, I knew it!" I was jumping up and down clapping my hands like I was at a football game! I looked down at Nicole's upside down face and she was laughing hysterically.

"Oh my God," she said. "I can't believe it, -- A boy!"

Dr. Johnson handed me the infant and said, "You can take him for a minute and then we need to warm him up and clean him." I cradled the prize and lowered him down into Nicole's arms. She looked at him the same way she had our other two children at birth and it was another moment I would never forget. Dr. Johnson called for him and we sent him back to get cleaned up. Nicole looked up at me.

"Sullivan Patrick!" she said.

"Yeah, we got our Sully!" I responded, and I gave her a kiss. "Are you okay?" I asked.

"Yeah, I'm fine."

"You sure?"

"Yes Ben."

"Okay, should I go make some calls and come right back?"

Nicole laughed, "Sure."

I looked at Nicole, and then looked up at the Russian. He nodded, "Go ahead," he said.

I ran out the double doors and down the hallway. My mother-in-law and sister-in-law were waiting there. "It's a boy!" I yelled, jumping up and down like a kid, and hugging my mother-in-law.

"I knew it too," she said. "I knew it had to be a boy!"

My sister-in-law seemed surprised because she thought it was a girl, but she was more humored by my jumping up and down near a full waiting room not, giving a shit who saw me! I never thought I would get one boy, let alone two. I was ecstatic and couldn't contain myself. I called my five year old daughter Milan, who like mommy, was expecting a girl. When I told her the news over the telephone she started crying and was like "Oh daddy that's great."

I knew where the conversation was headed so I said to her, "Mommy is so happy isn't this great?"

"Mommy is happy that it's a boy daddy?"

"Yeah honey, she thought it was a girl all along, but it's okay that it's a boy. It was a great surprise. Mommy is so happy right now!"

"Okay daddy. When do we get to see him?"

"Hi Daddy!" my three year old Preston yelled into the phone.

I heard a brief struggle for the phone back and forth between the two of them and finally they settled on holding the phone between them.

"When are we gonna see him Daddy?" asked Preston.

"Tomorrow guys. Eema and Opa are going to bring you to the hospital tomorrow morning to see him okay?"

"Okay daddy," they both said.

"Okay, I have to go take care of mommy and the baby. I'll see you guys in the morning. Be good okay?"

"Okay bye."

I sent out a text message blast to our friends, and I got a telephone call back from Nicole's best friend Danielle. She lived around the corner from the hospital and wanted to know if it was okay to come by and say hi. We had a history of not seeing eye-to-eye but it was often because my concern was misconstrued. Despite any differences I always had a fondness for her so I told her to come over.

I spent another twenty minutes making telephone calls to friends and relatives. "Yeah, hi! It's a boy! Sullivan Patrick arrived at eight o'clock. Eight pounds, and he's gorgeous."

I went back in to check on Nicole. They were almost finished with everything and were preparing to move her into the recovery room. "Okay, you can go into the recovery room next door and we'll bring your wife in shortly," said the Russian.

"Okay thanks," I said. I went back out the double doors and down the hallway to grab my mother-in-law and sister-in-law and bring them with me. Danielle was there with them and we all went back to the room. When we arrived Nicole was already there. Everyone exchanged hugs, and Nicole was thrilled to see Danielle. They held hands and tried to catch up on their busy lives in a New York minute, and as Nicole started to doze we began to chat amongst ourselves. When she fell asleep everyone left and I retreated to the waiting room. It was quiet and the lights were off. I was the only one in there at that late hour. I sat down exhausted and put my head down on the arm of the sofa. The soft glow of the exit lamp lit the artwork on the walls, and the soda machine hummed in the background. I wasn't sure what the next few days would bring. All of our kids were born with ABO blood incompatibility and so they were subject to jaundice and having to be under the lights. It wasn't life threatening, although Preston had it very bad. Preston also had a gray spell in the nursery and ended up in the NICU for ten days. It was brutal and we prayed that number three would not be that way.

The next day we got to spend time with the baby, and they started him under the photo-therapy lamps for the ABO jaundice. It would have been nice to come home the next day like normal people, but we were prepared for this. We ended up having to stay three days, and by the fourth day we were pretty well shot. Nicole and I sat in her room, tired, and wanting dearly to go home. We talked about how worn out we were from my surgery, our financial stress, and now the C-section.

"This is so painful. Do you think I'll ever be the same?" she asked.

"Yes Nicole, you'll be fine."

"No, I mean do you think my stomach will ever get flat again? Will I be able to run, and exercise, and wear a bathing suit?"

"Yes Nicole. I've told you this after each birth, and I've always been right. I'm going to tell you again. If you put in the effort, you can do anything you want with your body. Your body is a direct reflection of the effort you put into it." There was silence. Our eyes locked, and then we both turned toward the wall of windows overlooking Manhattan. Lights twinkled on a black backdrop, and sharp buildings pierced the night sky.

"Amazing right?"

"Yes it is," said Nicole. "I miss the city."

"Me too," I said. I grabbed her hand and we looked out the window together. It was beautiful. On that night the city looked like the Milky Way Galaxy. "So many good things have happened for me here in this city. When I moved here fourteen years ago it was the turning point in my life, and since then nothing but good things have happened for me here. I tell you what. I have an idea."

"What?" she asked.

"Do you want to run the New York City Marathon in November?"

"You just had open heart surgery five months ago, and I just had a C-section, is that a joke?"

"No it's not a joke. It's a possibility. Answer the question." Nicole had become an avid runner since she met me. She had dropped a lot of weight, become a healthy eater and really changed her life. I was proud of her and I always tried to offer support to keep her on that path. I knew that if I could get her to set a long term goal that it would keep her from getting post-partum depression. She never got depressed after having our other two children, but this time was going to be a lot more difficult for her because of the recovery from surgery, and everything else going on.

"Okay, sure. Let's run the NYC Marathon in November Ben," she said sarcastically.

"Great!" I said. "I'm glad you're on board. It will be on the one year anniversary of my open heart surgery. It will be a great way to celebrate, and it will give you something to focus on too so you don't get lazy and depressed." She looked at me like I was nuts, but I knew I had struck a chord with her.

On the day we were preparing to leave I got a chance to meet *Sarah Jessica Parker* in the nursery. Nicole and I were waiting for them to bring us Sully, and while we were standing there Nicole poked me and said "Did you see that?"

"What?" I asked.

"That was *Sarah Jessica Parker!*"

"No it wasn't, you're crazy."

"No Ben it really was. She had a baby here not too long ago. She loves this hospital."

"Okay whatever Nicole; can you go sign the papers so we can get out of here?" She left and waddled slowly down the hall to the nurses' station. I stayed at the nursery looking through the glass at Sully, marveling at how handsome he was. He looks perfect, like the Gerber baby. As I was standing there I turned away from the glass for a moment and saw *Sarah Jessica Parker* coming down the hall with a child and an older woman. At first I didn't recognize her, but I knew the face was familiar. I turned back to Sully behind the glass, and then I realized. *Holy shit, Nicole was right,* I thought. She got closer and I turned to her with a studly and vintage 1990s, "Hi... Congratulations."

"Hi there," she said. She approached the glass of the nursery. "Is that your baby?" Her voice is just as distinct as it was in *Sex in the City.*

I stood there mesmerized that this woman was not only saying hello to me, but gracing me with a conversation!

"Yyyyyeah, that's my baby," I said. I was dumbfounded and it felt like I was looking straight through her." I laughed and regained my focus. "Yes, that's my boy!"

"Well enjoy him. I have two at home and there's nothing like it. They're my pride and joy."

"Well thank you," I said with a big *Kool-Aid* smile. I saw Nicole coming down the hall behind her, and I chuckled. "I just want to say that my wife and I adore you. You are great."

"Thanks! Well, good luck. Enjoy."

"Nice meeting you," I said. I turned and Nicole was walking toward me smiling. She stopped at the reception desk and pointed at me, joking with the nurse.

"You see, I leave him alone for five minutes and look what he's up to!" We all laughed and with that the door to the nursery opened and Sully was wheeled out.

"Okay babe, they told me to go get the truck, and they'll bring you and Sully downstairs. I'll see you in a few minutes."

I went and got the truck, and within a few minutes we were packed in and headed back to Long Island. It was a smooth, peaceful ride. While we were at the hospital my mother-in-law was kind enough to go grocery shopping for us, and prepare the house for the baby. My mom had also come down to stay for a couple weeks to help Nicole get back on her feet and they were all waiting at the house for us. When we arrived there was an intimate greeting between Milan and Preston, and their new brother. I've never seen my daughter's eyes sparkle so much, and my son Preston was completely intrigued by how the little guy worked. They clearly had two different age and gender appropriate perceptions of their new brother. One seemed to look at him as her little baby doll to cuddle and nurture, and the other saw a moving, animated little creature that came out of his mommy's belly. The rest of that day and night was priceless. There was lots of questions, and cuddling on the couch.

The days that followed were skimp on sleep, and when my mother left it was even more brutal because I had to get up every time the baby cried and bring him to Nicole for breastfeeding. She wasn't able to get in and out of bed easily, so in addition to work and a four hour commute; I also had to do night duty. For at least the first month I walked around exhausted and relished when people visited because it was the only time I got sleep. I wouldn't have it any other way though. Burning the candle at both ends, and sacrificing to take care of your newborn is something that builds character. It's something you only get one chance to do with each child, and it bonds you to them in a special way. Memories are made that you will cherish for the rest of your life, and are far more valuable than photos, or videos. Those sleepless nights lying with your baby sleeping on your chest, or rocking in your arms are to die for. One night after Sully had woken up, I lay there in the dark with him on my bare chest. His warm cheek pressed against my surgery scar as he slept, and his rapid heartbeat buzzed in the background of my own. I could feel his tiny fingers touching my collarbone, and I watched his back rise and fall with each breath. It was the symphony of life.

After a few weeks Nicole started talking about getting back to the gym, and the Marathon. I had been going to the gym alone, but not with any consistency, so we started going together on weekends. We would grab coffee on the way and bring the kids because they had childcare and a big playroom. They seemed to enjoy the ritual as much as we did. It was slow going with the workouts. I was still on a couple of meds so I had to monitor my heart-rate closely, and Nicole had to use precautions because of the C-section. Besides not being able to push myself to the limit, the only problem I had was how exhausted I felt after the workouts. Sometimes the fatigue led into the next day and it affected my state-of-mind and ability to concentrate.

Neither Nicole nor I had ever run a marathon, but we were excited about our new goal of running the NYC Marathon in November. Registration was closed, but I did some research and was able to get us in by signing on with the American Heart Association and pledging to raise money for them. When people heard about our goal of running the Marathon so soon after heart surgery and childbirth, they were quick to question our sanity. They pointed out how challenging the feat was on a normal basis, let alone after surgery, with three kids, and a full-time job. What they didn't realize was that the challenge itself was part of the healing process for us. It was our way of fighting back against adversity and avoiding falling into the victims of circumstance role. We took control, giving our children a living example of how to bounce back from a setback.

August arrived, and up to that point we hadn't done much consistent training. We were on our way from the city to upstate New York for our annual family vacation at Ridin' Hy Dude Ranch. The kids had passed out asleep in the back seat, and Nicole and I were catching up on life.

"You know, we only have about three months left before the Marathon. We really need to start training. These weekend visits to the gym running on the treadmill aren't going to cut it. Sal is already doing nine mile runs," said Nicole.

"That's great," I said. "I'm not worried about it. We'll start soon."

"That's fine Ben, but not everyone has your confidence. I really need to get some training under my belt. We're going to start today."

"Today?"

"Yes. It's perfect! We can run in the horse trails and your mom can watch the kids while we go." How could I argue with her?

"Okay. That sounds good," I said.

Most people rest on vacation, but Nicole and I have always enjoyed working out together and vacation was one of the few times we could do so in a relaxed environment. When we arrived at the dude ranch the kids went buck wild as usual. They ran to the shuffle board, to the beach, and then to the game room. It was heaven for them, and equally enjoyable for us. There was so much for them to do and so many people to help keep an eye on them that Nicole and I always got to enjoy some adult time together. After our afternoon horseback ride we got changed into our running gear and turned the kids over to my mother. We hit the road and brought my eleven year old nephew Ethan on the run with us on his insistence. I wanted to run on the trails but Nicole was nervous about getting trampled by horses, so we agreed to run on the dirt roads instead. The countryside was beautiful, but after the first car passed and we choked on road dust she too thought it might be better to run on the horse trails next time! Since we didn't know where we were going or have any idea of mileage we decided to just run for a half hour. The roads were very hilly, and I was feeling sluggish immediately. I was so out of shape. At one point during the run I felt a frightening heart palpitation. Since my surgery any little flutter of my heart, even the slightest gas pain frightened the hell out of me. The doctor said they were not related to the surgery, but they still got my attention in a way they never did before. I enjoyed running with Nicole. She was a soccer all-star in high school, but never did any consistent running. When we first met I was doing a lot of running and weight training and she started joining me on the runs. Ironically, as my dedication waned over the years, she turned into a galloping nut! She had taken a strong liking to it, and it was nice to see all of the positive things the sport had given her. She was determined to get back in shape and had done more training than I over the past month so I found myself struggling to keep up with her. I kept teasing her to enjoy the dominance because it wouldn't last long. We ran for twenty-four minutes and the last half mile of the run was up a progressively steep hill. I had to use every ounce of willpower to not walk up the hill. I could hear myself telling my six year old daughter that it's okay to run as slow as you want as long as you don't walk. I purposely leaned my arm and bodyweight on Nicole going up the hill to slow her down and we both laughed. Running was different after surgery because I was always having thoughts of dropping dead during the workout. It's morbid, but I think it's only human to have those thoughts after an event like I had been through. I pushed on though. As my favorite rapper once said, *I'd rather die like a man, than live like a coward.*"

Later that night after a long day of swimming, horseback riding, and waterskiing our family gathered in the lodge to listen to live country music and dance. After a couple of hours I retreated to the fireplace with my laptop. The fireplace was in the main room of the lodge where huge rustic beams crossed overhead. I sat in an overstuffed chair near the crackling fire, where deer and bear head hung, looking down from the stone wall above me. As I stared idly at the computer screen reflecting on the day, I decided it was a perfect time to start the blog that I had been procrastinating about. I wanted to start a blog to increase awareness about aortic aneurysms, and to be a touchstone for people going through open heart surgery. John Ritter died because of the lack of awareness on aortic aneurysms, and because I nearly fell prey to the same circumstances I felt compelled to get the word out, clear up any fears or misconceptions, and give people a place to go for firsthand experience and inspiration. That night I started *Heartosaurus.com*. Over the next few months it would serve as a place for me to share my struggles and achievements; healing, while helping others.

When we returned home, we continued the "stepped up" training we had started at the dude ranch, and by the end of August we had built up to a six mile run. We also registered for the *Great Cow Harbor Race* in Northport, NY. It was to be held at the end of September and would serve as a stepping stone to the marathon helping to keep us motivated.

On September 6th we did our longest run yet; a ten miler. Considering the length of the run I felt relatively good on all accounts. Any aches and pains were not related to my heart surgery and I was grateful for that. The only thing that bothered me was my right hamstring which I had strained the previous week. I had mapped out the run, but never run it before. There was a very steep climb at about mile six and it hit us like a ton of bricks! Nicole experienced a bout of tourettes-like sarcasm three quarters of the way up the hill and started yelling at me. "This was real smart," she said, as if I had purposely put the hill there to piss her off, and mapped out the run that way! I ran ahead and when she got to the top I growled out one of my typical *get diesel* speeches. There was another hill shortly after, that was not quite as steep, but it was long and drawn out, and the only way I made it without walking was fixating on Nicole. I got yelled at for "crowding" her into the gutter but when she realized I was pacing off her because I was hurting so badly she softened up. I couldn't believe how much of a machine she had turned into. She won some local road races in her age group the previous year, but with more training I felt like she could win some major ones. She hadn't yet realized the depth of her own talent, often limiting herself. She had become pretty good for someone who simply started running for fitness with me ten years ago. When we finished the run I was completely drained. I walked over to the front porch and dropped my butt onto the step; my legs no longer able to support my weight. I sat there for a good twenty minutes, too stiff and tired to move.

As the month progressed I pushed myself harder and harder on the training runs in preparation for the Cow Harbor race. I began to think about what my marathon time would be and asked God to help me complete it. I continued to chase Nicole on most of the runs, and as the intensity and length of our workouts increased I found myself having more anxiety of "popping a hose" or something far-fetched happening to my newly repaired heart. All of it was psychological, as cardiovascularly I felt like a million bucks. A week before the Cow Harbor race I had the pleasure of meeting the people from the John Ritter Foundation and they ran a short story on their network about my website and marathon mission. Afterward Nicole and I decided to have *Heartosaurus - In Memory of John Ritter* jerseys made up for the race. We couldn't wait until the end of the month.

Funerals aren't scheduled.

I **WAS IN HOME DEPOT** with my wife and three kids getting a replacement doorknob. I prefer to visit Home Depot alone, but more often than not I have some or all of the family with me because it's usually a stop in between soccer games, grocery shopping or another family affair. It's always an experience, mostly because my three year old Preston acts up. It's as if he gets a whiff of the testosterone in the air and he's off! I've never seen anything like it. The moment this kid enters Home Depot it's as if he knows it is a man's haven! I plead until I'm blue in the face for him to stay by my side, but it never lasts for more than a moment. "Put down the light bulbs! Take that rope off your legs! GET OFF OF THAT LADDER!"

One time he took off running like a bat out of hell up and down the aisles. He was so far ahead that I couldn't catch him. I could not stop laughing, trying to catch the little madman. There we went up and down the aisles; the spiky haired kid with the devilish smile running all out with dad in hot pursuit like *Forrest Gump*. In my peripheral vision I could see customers with amused faces whizzing by, and employees with looks of astonishment. I'm sure it was quite the spectacle to them, considering that not only was the misbehaved kid laughing, but the parent in chase was also hysterical. I put on an angry face every time he looked back, but I couldn't help laughing out loud when his back was turned. At one point I stopped chasing and shortly after found him standing in the front of the store looking around and panting. He was terrified because he was lost. I peeked around the corner and when he saw me he smiled and bolted for the next aisle but I was too close and I tackled him.

During the visit we stopped in the window and door department and I asked for Brian McAvey. He was a salesman that I had become very close to while building my own home. I hadn't seen him in a long time because my house was finished and I had not been in the store as often. He was very knowledgeable not only about windows, doors, and home building; but also in finance, politics, and life. It was odd that I had gotten to know all this about him just from frequenting the store, but he was a man's man; one of those guys that you just enjoyed talking to. He was impressed that I had taken on building a house with no prior experience in the building trades and I was intrigued by his background and tremendous success in business. He had done very well for himself in the insurance business and was merely working at Home Depot as a hobby to get himself out of the house during retirement. He didn't need the money. He and I designed the tremendous wall of windows in the back of my great room from scratch. I took the measurements he needed, and he drew the entire plan out on graph paper. He created an architectural masterpiece including French panes in each window that lined up perfectly. It was a complex undertaking, one that I would have paid an architect a few thousand bucks for, but Brian offered his expertise free of charge and it turned out to be one of the most admired areas of our home. He was influential and helped me with many other important details and planning during the project. In addition to all of his help and expertise, he happened to be one of the nicest people I had ever met. We shared a demented sense of humor, good family values, and he was always social with my family when they accompanied me to the store.

"I'm sorry to have to tell you this, but Brian died last year," said the salesman behind the desk as he was working with another customer. He didn't even turn away from the computer as he spoke. He just typed and looked straight ahead at the computer monitor as he told me this bad news.

"What?" I said.

"What happened?" said my wife.

"Yeah, he had a heart attack and dropped dead instantly right on the floor in the store."

"You're joking right?" I asked. *Salesmen, especially good ones were known for having a demented sense of humor, and I was waiting for Brian to walk out from behind one of the aisles.*

"You're serious," I said.

"Yes, unfortunately I am. I wouldn't joke about that. I'm sorry to have to tell you that."

"I can't believe it. Oh my God. Wow, he was such a good man. That's horrible. I feel so bad."

I got choked up and blood rushed to my face. Nicole and I looked at each other and I could tell the news upset her too. We stood there awkwardly for a moment, as our son pulled on every doorknob in the aisle behind us.

"Yep, he didn't smoke or anything; a regular jogger. And yes, you're right; he was a good person."

The salesman pointed me in the direction of the doorknob I needed, and for the rest of the day and night that conversation haunted me. I thought about Brian over and over and felt so sad. I thought about his family and the stories he told me about them. He was proud of his kids and his wife who was a high powered local attorney.

Hearing about Brian's death after what I had just been through caught me off guard and was particularly disturbing. He was healthy and died of a heart attack which immediately caused me to think of an aortic aneurysm and dissection. The timing of this news was warped. I hadn't seen him in over a year, but my life went on during that time. I guess I expected his had too. I expected him to be there in the window and door department sitting at the desk like a permanent fixture in the store; waiting to rub my son on the head and help me with the problem of the day. I expected to pick up where we left off, and I was shook when I found out otherwise. That could have been me last year if my aortic aneurysm ruptured or my surgery went bad. It could be me tomorrow; it could be you, it could be anyone!

You don't get an invitation when it's time. You don't get anything that says "Hey, Bob is going to keel over at 7:00 p.m. on June 23, would you attend? And by the way, if there's anything you need to say or do with him before hand then please do so." People live everyday thinking there is a long future. They don't say things that are on their mind thinking they'll have time later. Some say or do things they regret, and think they'll have time to make up for them tomorrow. People live "the daily grind" with no real consideration for the people and details around them. They put things off for another day, and they are consumed with the minutiae of everyday life. Why? One of the biggest reasons is because they don't see an "end." If they did, perhaps they would treat life more delicately. Anyone who's had to look death in the face has a different perspective. This unique perspective is a common denominator that bonds survivors together whether it is from cancer, heart disease, a car accident or anything else.

Like the *Tim McGraw* song *Live Like you were Dying;*

You never know when God will tap you. Tell your wife, and kids, and even the guy at Home Depot who was so kind to you how great they are.

In Memory of John Ritter.

THE *GREAT COW HARBOR RACE* is a 10k run along the harbor in Northport Village and there were a bunch of activities, festivals, and parties associated with it. ESPN ranks it as one of the top 100 runs in the USA, and Nicole and I were excited to be running in it. We had a pasta dinner planned for the night before the race and a big bonfire celebration afterwards. My brother-in-law James and sister-in-law Michelle came in for the weekend to run with the kids in the fun run while we competed in the main race. Milan and Preston had done races with us in the past, but they were particularly interested in participating in this one because of the underlying meaning to us as a family.

On race day we were all up at the crack of dawn. A cup of coffee later we were at the starting line. The crowd of spectators and runners at the starting line grew so quickly that you couldn't walk around without bumping into people. Our friends the Stearns had a house right on the starting line, so we gathered there with friends and family waiting for the start of the race. A band played, people mingled, and then the final moment came. Nicole and I lined up with everyone on the starting line and bid our kids good luck in their fun run. We gave each other a quick pound and the gun went off to a stampede of footsteps and cheering. Nicole had been beating me up in training, but for a change I set the pace in the race. It was disgustingly hot and humid, but I felt great.

"I feel like a million bucks!" I said to Nicole who was running beside me. She was not one for conversation during a race and just nodded. At mile four she dropped off pace and I started getting on her case.

"Let's go Nicole!" I said, "Get up here!" She jogged miserably behind me.

"Nicole what the hell are you doing, you said you wanted to break fifty minutes and I'm trying to keep us on pace! I don't understand, you always outrun me in training." She was quiet and didn't say anything and I began to get annoyed.

"Let's Go Nicole!" I yelled again.

"I can't! I think I just got my period."

"Are you serious?" I asked.

"No Ben I'm kidding."

I shook my head and ran next to her. There was a brief silence, and then I looked over at her with a smile.

"Well you have black tights on, so you can't see anything." I laughed. She looked at me with dismay.

"What?" I asked.

"Just go ahead of me, I can't do it. I'm going to stop."

"No Nicole, I'm not doing that."

"Just go Ben!"

"No Nicole. If you don't run with me and finish with me I'm not doing the marathon with you in November." I didn't think she was lying about getting her period, but I knew that wasn't what was affecting her running. She was just having a bad run, and I needed to pull her through it. Having an "off" day was familiar to all runners and I knew she just needed a push to get through the race and finish. With a mile and a half left I looked at my watch and saw that we had fallen off pace, but I didn't want to leave her. It was her who pulled me through all the training and everything else in life, convincing me to train on days when I questioned the marathon goal. We came down the hill into the final stretch and we could see the finish line. I reached out my hand and we ran the last 100 meters together, and gave each other a big hug as we came through the finish. We did it in 53 minutes, and all things considered; gave ourselves the confidence boost we needed to continue on to the NYC marathon. It wasn't the sub-50 time that we wanted, but it also wasn't a perfect race. I was thrilled at how great I felt during and after the race. It seemed easy. We met up with our family and the kids at the end of the finish line chute, and walked around the runner's expo. Then we all went to breakfast. Ten or fifteen of us sat in the outdoor garden of a diner in the quaint village of Northport, and as I looked around the table I was grateful to be in such good company, and to be alive.

I had kept in touch with my surgeon long after my operation. We had established an uncommon bond afterward, one in which he would send an occasional email or text message to check in on me; and I would harass him about running the marathon with me. He had done a triathlon with one of his former patients, so I kept trying to talk him in to running the marathon with me. As the race got closer I wanted to get checked by him to make sure everything was intact for the race. I emailed him one day, and asked if he would check me out. He replied back promptly and said no problem that I could call his assistant Debra and she would get me in.

"Hi Debra, this is Benjamin Carey, Dr. Stewart's patient," I said.

"Yes, hi Benjamin, how are you?"

"I'm doing great. Dr. Stewart said I should call you to schedule a checkup with him."

"Yes, he wants you to come in for an echocardiogram and then meet with him afterwards. Let me.....wait hold on."

There was silence on the line, and then a familiar voice; "How you feeling? Are you getting soft on me? How's the heart holding up?" asked Dr. Stewart. I laughed. It was so typical for him to just pick up the phone on a call to his office and start talking as if an old friend. He had done it numerous times on calls my wife and I had made and it was a tribute to his down to earth personality. He was such a congenial guy. Most top heart surgeons were known for having big egos and stifled personalities. Dr. Stewart was the rare breed who had the whole package.

"I'm doing great," I said. "I just need you to double check your work and make sure nothing is coming loose." He chuckled. "So are you going to run with me or what?" I asked. "You did a triathlon; now let's see if you can get through 26 miles!"

"Uhhhh....I don't really run," he said. "Not that long anyway."

"Excuses," I said.

"Okay," he said. "People are going to think this is a joke when they hear about it, but see if you can get me in and I'll do it with you."

"What?" I asked.

"Get me into the marathon and I'll do it. I think registration is closed, but if you can get me in I'll do it," he said.

"Deal," I said. "I suggest you start training so I don't kick your ass too bad." He laughed at me.

"I'm putting Debra back on to schedule you."

"Okay thanks," I said.

I made small talk with Debra when she got back on the phone, and she scheduled me for my pre-race checkup and echo for October 22nd; a few weeks before the marathon. I was relieved that Dr. Stewart was going to run the marathon with me. I gave him a hard time on our phone call, but the reality is that I wanted to know he was nearby in case anything happened to me. I realized that even if something did happen, having him around wouldn't necessarily save me, but it definitely gave me peace of mind and eased my anxiety.

The next day I reached out to the NYRR club to inquire about Dr. Stewart running with me in the race. I got back a very unexpected response from their in-house counsel questioning my condition to be running the race a year after open heart surgery. The serious and formal tone of the email was alarming, and it seemed like they were threatening to revoke my registration because I was a medical risk. They asked for a statement from me as to why they should allow me to run, what kind of training I had done, and if I could get statements from my doctors clearing me to participate. I responded to the email with a full log of my training, and pointed out that people had competed in past marathons with more serious conditions than mine. Within a week I had convinced them that I was healthy enough to run, and they also extended special late entry to Dr. Stewart so that he could run. I was ecstatic. I emailed Dr. Stewart with the news, and he sent back a sarcastic response about how thrilled he was to be running 26.2 miles. I broke his chops a little more and then told him I would see him on the 22nd for my checkup.

On the morning of October 22nd I headed into the city for an EKG at *New York-Presbyterian hospital*. I had been feeling melancholy as it got closer to November 2nd, the one year anniversary of my open heart surgery. The colder weather, change of seasons, my grandmother's memory, and Halloween approaching all reminded me vividly of what I had gone through at the same time the previous year. I thought about how frightened and anxious I was the year before and was grateful that everything turned out okay. On arrival at the hospital I recognized the same enormous poster of a Yankees player hanging in front of the Millstein building; reminding passersby of their patient roster, and elite status of the hospital. A sense of calm and serenity overcame me when I arrived. It was odd, and hard to explain, but I realized for the first time what my friend Ken meant back when he referred to his own heart experience as a "bittersweet" time. He had the same procedure a couple of years before me, and was a big support when I was diagnosed with the same condition. When he spoke about his open heart surgery he glowed, and I could never understand why he didn't think it was the worst thing in the world like I did. I thought it was weird, but now I could understand his perspective perfectly. It's easy to comprehend for anyone who has lived through a major operation or faced a terminal illness. Everything becomes overwhelming and larger than life; so much so that you are forced to "let go, and let God." Afterward, if you are lucky enough to survive; you associate feelings of complete serenity with the experience. It's as if you and the earth and God were one for that moment in time; and you made it to see another day. As I was standing at the check-in desk in the main lobby of the hospital, my mind began to wander. I gazed at the familiar coffee bar, and had a flashback of Nicole and me making a quick stop there at 5:00 a.m. on the morning of my surgery; two terrified soul mates, fearing the unknown.

I arrived at the sonogram department in the hospital. The woman at the check-in desk was very friendly and chatted me up. I still didn't get it; were they paying these people triple the wages of other hospitals? Even the service from the receptionist was over the top. It was early in the morning, and the place was already busy, yet she managed to handle my check-in with unexpected kindness. In most other hospitals you were lucky to be acknowledged. I had seen receptionists that purposely buried their heads in paperwork to avoid having to speak to patients that approached the desk. A few minutes passed and the sonogram tech arrived and took me to the room. I was very nervous during the scan, but the woman was also very social, putting me at ease. She was also very knowledgeable describing everything she was doing, and answering the dozens of questions I asked in detail. I had prior experiences with sonograms and CT scans at other places where you were treated like cattle on an assembly line.

After the sonogram I went up to Dr. Stewart's office. I was sitting in the waiting room outside of his office and the woman at the desk offered me a cup of coffee. While I was sitting there sipping on my coffee a woman in a white lab coat walked past. She glanced at me and then did a double take. She approached me smiling.

"Hi, aren't you Benjamin?"

I was taken totally off guard and smirked. "Yes, I am," I said.

"How are your wife and baby? I remember she was pregnant when you were here before your operation."

"They're doing well! Wow, you remembered that?" I asked. I couldn't believe it. *You couldn't make this shit up!* I thought. The people at New York-Presbyterian were just so damn friendly and down to earth.

"Sure I remember. You were pretty nervous about having surgery. Anyway, I'm glad things are good. Have a nice day."

"Thanks, you too," I said, smiling.

About a half hour later Dr. Stewart called me in. I had a very quick meeting with him in which he told me everything looked great. I didn't want to take up too much of his time because I assumed his daily schedule was chock full, but I wanted to feel reassured that everything was going to be okay with my heart for the marathon.

"No issues?" I asked.

"No. Nothing," he said. "Everything looks good."

"Are you sure?"

He laughed. "Yes," he said, going into a much more detailed explanation of the integrity of the valve and other factors that he knew would appease me. We then exchanged stories about our marathon training, and talked about how behind we both were. We joked about not being able to finish.

"Well alright then. I guess I'll see you in a couple of weeks," I said. "Don't come up with any excuses before then," I joked. I left feeling energized; the same way I always felt after a meeting with him. He was more than just my surgeon, he had become a good friend; someone who inspired me to go beyond.

A week before the marathon I was not sleeping well. I was having a lot of nightmares, and not feeling rested in the morning. I was having vivid recollections of what was going on last year in those last days before my procedure, and it was sapping my energy. It was as if my body was having a physiological and subconscious response to the time of year. I couldn't figure it out, but I was being drawn to anything that brought me back to the surgery; like a moth to a flame. I began napping in the Montauk room, and spending time in the red chair near the fireplace where I spent most of my recovery the previous year. Was it cell memory? Was my body biologically remembering the trauma? Perhaps the change of seasons, foliage, cold weather, and all of the other sensory reminders have caused it. Maybe it was my visit back to the hospital that brought it on.

I spent Halloween carving pumpkins with the kids, trick-or-treating, watching football, and having a great home cooked meal by my mother-in-law. I had strained my calf in training, and was nervous about the marathon the following week. My distance base had suffered as a result of the injury, and I wasn't feeling confident. Originally I wanted to break four hours for the marathon, but going into the last week I was praying just to finish. At the end of the day Nicole and I sat on the brown leather sofa near the potbelly woodstove in our library. The walls are walnut, almost black, and books line shelves from floor to ceiling. Shade covered wall sconces cast a soft glow in the room. A wrought iron chandelier with matching shades hangs, reflecting onto the silver tin ceiling above. Nicole was reading a book, and I sat quietly next to her, tracing the pink veins in the shiny marble floor with my big toe. My eyes began to follow the brass nail heads outlining the chair across from me as I drifted off into thought. *How fortunate was I not only to be alive, but healthy enough to be training for a marathon?* I thought about all of the family and friends who came over on Halloween the year before to see me one last time before my operation. We were fortunate, and I remembered every last gesture and act of kindness; even from the people who simply had the courtesy to ask how things were going during a time when a simple question like that brightened our days. People continued to make donations to the American Heart Association charity that we were running for, and we entered our final days before the marathon.

November 2, 2010

What a Difference a Year Makes.

ONE YEAR AGO I WOKE UP AT 4:00 A.M. to travel in to NYC for a scheduled open heart surgery. Our close friend Danielle Macagnone got up in the middle of the night to drive us in and drop us off and ensure that we weren't stressed out any more than necessary. My family followed, and I had valve-sparing open heart surgery to cut out an ascending aortic aneurysm and replace the diseased aorta and underscore of the aortic arch. Not only was the surgery itself an overwhelming experience; but the days leading up to the surgery, and the days since took on a new meaning. I had gone to bed and woken up for thirty-six years and assumed life would go on, but then at thirty-seven years old I was suddenly facing my own mortality. It's amazing how we wake up every day and just take for granted that life will go on. We know the reality that it will end at some point, yet we still wake up every morning believing deeply, that we will live forever. My experience has kept the finitude of life fresh in my mind. I don't miss an opportunity to say thank you, to show gratitude, or tell someone that I love them because you never know when it may be your last chance to do it.

A COUPLE OF DAYS BEFORE THE MARATHON I had my last examination by my cardiologist Dr. Walsh. He was very conservative and had asked me to come in for a second visit in less than a month to make sure everything was working properly with my heart before the race. He called in the best technician in the hospital to come and personally perform the final EKG on me, and he scrutinized it. Finally he gave me a firm handshake and clean bill of health and wished me good luck in the race. His wonderful team of ladies working in the office asked me to send their regards to my wife and children, and they too wished me good luck in the marathon on Sunday. I drove home with a renewed confidence that I was going to be strong for my race. It was cold and rainy outside and I stared straight ahead through the wipers sweeping the raindrops back and forth on the windshield in a steady rhythm. My cell phone rang and it was Nicole. "Guess what," she said.

"What?" I asked.

"Jay and Tracey

Kufeld are sending us VIP finish line tickets for our parents."

"No way, what do you mean?"

"Yeah, Jay does business with NYRR and said he's sending over the passes."

"Nicole that is hundreds of dollars we're talking about."

"Yeah I know; aren't they awesome?"

"Wow. Please give them my regards, and thanks. They're great," I said. "That was so nice of them. We're lucky to have such good friends Nicole."

"I know. They're the best," she said. "I'll see you when you get home."

We made plans to stay overnight in the city the night before the marathon with our close friends Sal and Ali. Sal was running the NYC Marathon too for the first time and all of our families were planning on meeting in the city the next day to cheer us on. My sister-in-law was going to watch the kids for us the entire day, and I had taken Monday off from the office in case I couldn't walk. We picked up some energy gel packs to eat during the run, a new pacing watch, and some power bars. We also had commemorative jerseys made up for the race that had my *Heartosaurus.com* logo on it, and a tribute to John Ritter and my heart surgeon printed on the back. By Friday our excitement was spilling over and we couldn't wait to race on Sunday.

"Yay, Opa and Eema are here!" my kids yelled as they ran to the front door. "Opa" is German for grandpa, and "Eema" is a name given to my mother by my daughter when she was a baby and couldn't pronounce grandma. It was Saturday morning the day before the marathon. I looked out the window in the front of the house and saw my stepdad Ed fighting awkwardly to pull a huge green board out of the car. As he pulled it out he almost fell over in the driveway, and my mom shook her head laughing and headed up to our door. "Go Team Carey" was printed on the green board in big bold letters. It was a huge sign that he had made. In fact, when he came inside we saw that he made two of them, made a map of the race course with pushpins to track us, and had his phone and Ipad all set up to track us electronically. He is the best! We spent the rest of the day relaxing with my parents and the kids, and then prepared to head into the city to have dinner with Sal and Ali and get a good night's sleep before the race.

We listened to Baroque music on the drive into the city. It was relaxing to have time alone after a busy week. The skyline of twinkling city lights expanded on us as we got closer to the Mid-Town Tunnel and that familiar feeling of being home hit us. Like a scene out of a 3-D movie, we drove out of the tunnel and into the city. The streets were bustling with throngs of people there for the marathon. We drove down to Ali and Sal's place in SoHo and parked near our favorite café, *La Lanterna de Vittorio*. As we walked by, Nicole and I got melancholy about the many romantic nights we spent there listening to opera near the fireplace and sharing French cheeses and tiramisu. *La Lanterna* wasn't a full-fledged restaurant, but was one of those late night places you ended up at after a movie or dancing. The best thing about it was that it was tucked away in an understated brownstone. There was no real signage, and if you didn't know it was there you would walk right past it. It was a speakeasy sort of place and had a cult following. On the way to Sal and Ali's we passed an authentic Belgian waffle place. My mouth watered and I made a mental note of its location.

When we arrived, our friends were happy to see us. We didn't get to see each other frequently, but there was no question of the bond between us. Nicole had gone to grade school with Ali. She is very petite and pretty, with long brown hair and a soft raspy voice. Sal is a clean cut guy originally from Philadelphia, and his PA character remained unspoiled by Wall Street. He is one of those guys you meet and within the first five minutes of meeting him you know he's someone you want in your corner. They were a fixture at every major Carey event and we regarded them as family. They were present for the birth of all three of our babies, and they also visited me in the hospital the day after I had my heart surgery.

We spent most of the evening in the kitchen; the four of us making a delicious pasta and chicken dinner. Their apartment is a quaint triplex, with hardwood floors and a wrought iron spiral staircase. It is tastefully appointed with avant-garde décor, and a door opens off of the living room onto a small balcony overlooking New York University. As we cooked *Ben Harper* played in the background, and garlic simmered in olive oil. Ali sliced an onion, and Nicole stirred linguini. Four friends brought each other up to speed on their busy lives, while toasting wineglasses and eating brie and crackers. When conversation about family, work, and vacations waned, we started going over our marathon strategies and expectations. Dr. Stewart and I were scheduled to be interviewed early in the morning before the race so we decided that we would take the 7:00 a.m. ferry over to the starting line in Staten Island. I was humored by how stressed out Nicole and Sal were getting about the "when and where" of taking their gels and eating their power bars during the race. Eating them was proven to extend your energy and prevent you from hitting the wall, but I just didn't think a couple of gel packs were going to help my own sorry ass across the finish line. We got all of our gear set up for the next morning, made final phone calls, and gave Ali our bags to bring to the restaurant we were meeting everyone at after the race. She was also going to hand us power bars if we needed them at around mile seventeen when we passed by our family cheering station at 73rd street. All in all, we had a wonderful and relaxing night. It was perfect. Before my head hit the pillow I got a text message from my primary doctor, Mark Singer, wishing me good luck the next day. He was the one who sent me for my stress test that diagnosed my aneurysm the year before. In a weird twist, he too was running the marathon. What were the chances I would be running the NYC Marathon a year after having open heart surgery, with two of the doctors that saved my life? I was nervous as I retired for the night. Nicole fell asleep shortly before I did. I lay awake asking God to ensure that my body handled everything with grace the next day, and that I would remain stable afterwards. A week before the marathon I had read about how the stress of a marathon temporarily damages your heart tissue, and about a guy who keeled over a few days after he completed a marathon. I was sure that there was a better chance of being struck by lightning, but nonetheless I was a little psyched out.

The real glory is being knocked to your knees

and then coming back. That's real glory.

That's the essence of it.

-Vince Lombardi

MY EYES OPENED and I turned over and rustled Nicole. "Wake up, we need to get moving," I said.

"Okay, okay," said Nicole. And she just laid there sleeping.

"Get up!" I poked her in the ribs.

"Okay Ben! I'm up, I'm up!" We both got up and started getting dressed. We could hear Sal in the kitchen downstairs making us his trademark race day breakfast which consisted of oatmeal, granola, yogurt, and some fruit. Ali was the cutest thing moping around in her pajamas squinting and trying to get everything together that she needed to take to the finish line for us. She had a sleepy hoarseness in her voice as she went through her checklist to make sure we were all ready and hadn't forgotten anything. We sat at the table eating breakfast together, still talking about our strategies for the marathon. Sal and Nicole seemed to have theirs down to a science, and every time I came up with one of my own I changed it. "I'll just be glad to finish," I said, and we all laughed.

After breakfast we packed up and headed out. We wore old sweatshirts and hats to keep us warm until the start of the race, and our plan was to just ditch everything and leave it behind at the starting line. We grabbed a cab that took us to Battery Park where we boarded the ferry to take us to Staten Island. The NYC Marathon was 26.2 miles and the course ran through all five boroughs. It started in Staten Island, went through Brooklyn, into Queens, next into Manhattan, briefly into the Bronx, and then finished in Manhattan's Central Park. The ferry ride was quiet, and from inside the boat we watched the sun come up. It looked to be a gorgeous day. The three of us sat there as the boat rocked gently back and forth and the morning rays of the sun warmed us. Nicole and Sal chatted about the race, and I slowly drifted into my own thoughts until their conversation became muffled, and finally silent. I looked over at them and their mouths kept moving but there was silence. I turned away to look out the window and watched the bow of the boat gently cover the sun with the ebb and flow of each wave. Coincidentally it was around this time last year that Sal and Ali Merlino, my parents, my wife, and Dr. Stewart were all in the same building at *New York-Presbyterian* hospital in Manhattan. I, lying on a stretcher maxed out on morphine with tubes and wires coming out all over, running a very different race; and they at my bedside. Who would have thought we would all be coming together a year later in the same great city to run a marathon? It would have seemed silly, if not impossible at the time. I set out on the mission for a number of reasons, but at the deepest level I wanted to run out of true grit, and defiance of giving in and letting my open heart surgery get the best of me. It was about "living", not merely ticking away the minutes of a life in existence. I wanted to be an example of strength for my children to look back on, and remember the year of adversity that preceded the Marathon. I was running to spread the word about my blog, and to create awareness about aortic disease to save lives. I was running in memory of John Ritter whose passing had shown the importance of proper screening and preventative care of aortic disease. John died, but his brother, I and others had lived because of him. I knew that I would be in Staten Island shortly, preparing to get through 26.2 miles. I guessed that it would take me about four and a half hours to complete the race. I thought it was roughly the amount of time I spent with Dr. Stewart and Nicole by my side last year on the operating table.

"Let's go," Nicole blurted out in her sharp, stereotypically loud Italian voice breaking the silence of my daydreaming. Sal and I looked at each other and the three of us started laughing. We unloaded from the ferry and as we walked up the steep ramp NYRR volunteers directed us where to go, and shouted hoots and hollers of good luck. Our zigzagging parade of runners made its way to a line of shuttle buses that would bring us to the starting line which was a couple of miles away. We sat in the front of the bus so that we could get off first. I had no idea where the hell we were or where we were going. All I knew about Staten Island was that it was built on a dump and the mafia lived there. The ride didn't take more than ten minutes and it brought us to the staging area for the race. Because there were so many thousands of people running, the start of the NYC Marathon was a spectacle and marvel in itself. There were different waves of runners that went off at staggered times to avoid people trampling each other, and amazingly every year things went off without a hitch. As we got off the bus the crowd was sheer madness. There were about a hundred porta-potties lined up, runners all over the place, and over fifty tents pitched. There were sports tents, medical tents, information tents, coffee booths, you name it. I said to Sal and Nicole, "Guys I'm supposed to meet Dr. Stewart at the main medical tent for an interview." They both looked at the mad scene in front of us and chuckled.

"Okay let's go," they said. We spent about the next forty-five minutes going to at least four different medical tents to find Dr. Stewart and the press team that wanted to interview us, and had no luck finding anyone. It was naïve to think we would find each other in the chaos, but we were all running for the first time and had no idea what to expect. To make matters worse, none of us carried a cell phone because no one wanted to carry it for 26.2 miles. The only things to be carried were gel packs and a power bar. As we walked around we grabbed a bagel and coffee, a bottle of water, and used the bathrooms for the last time. We weren't able to find Dr. Stewart but I didn't feel so bad. He made it clear that he was not going to be running at our pace for 26.2 miles anyway. The point that he was running the race at all gave me inspiration and peace of mind even if I couldn't see him.

"Blue Wave Two, Final Call!" the announcer said. With that we made a bee line to our staging area. It was the funniest thing I'd ever seen in a race. They had all of us herded like cattle into these winding chutes leading to the starting line. I started getting butterflies. It was a glorious day. It was crisp and cold, but not bitter. The morning sun was bright in the clear blue sky, and geese flew overhead in a "V" formation. Our wave slowly made its way up to the starting line. As we got closer the three of us stripped off our heavy sweat suits and tossed them to the side like everyone else. Apparently NYRR collected the discarded clothing and donated it to charity. I started bouncing up and down to get my legs loose. Sal plugged into his Ipod, and Nicole just smiled at us. Nicole and I planned to run the whole race together, but I joked with her that if she got soft on me like she did in Cow Harbor I might leave her in Brooklyn. Sal had put together a better training base than we did, and although we felt we would all run about the same pace; we didn't want to hold him back if anything went wrong. We hadn't gotten to the level of training that we wanted to be at for the race, and our confidence was a little low. We walked the final few hundred feet of the staging chute to the starting line which was at the beginning of the Verrazano Bridge. Helicopters chopped the air above us and a newscaster stood on top of a huge television news truck making announcements. The national anthem was played and immediately afterward thousands of runners began to cheer. *Frank Sinatra* played

"New York, New York" on huge loudspeakers overhead. Runners sang along, cheered, and prepared for the gun. Nicole and I gave Sal a hug and we all wished each other good luck. We jumped up and down, psyched for the start. I looked straight ahead at the Verrazano Bridge shining in the sun and my thoughts drowned out the chaos around me. I thought about my children at home and I couldn't wait to start running. The gun went off and people screamed and cheered. TV cameras were everywhere and there were so many people running at the same time that it felt like a stampede. My heart raced with adrenaline and it felt great. Nicole and I ran side by side along the Verrazano Bridge with thousands of people. All you heard were millions of footsteps and occasional hoots and hollers of excitement. I looked up at the soaring peaks of the bridge on that beautiful sunny day, and all I could think of was lying in that hospital bed last year; lifeless, and half conscious on morphine. "How the hell did I make it from there to here?" I asked myself. I looked over at Nicole running next to me, Sal in front of me, and thought about Dr. Stewart behind me. Then I thought about our friends and family on the sidelines, and the ones watching us on TV at home. That answered my question.

My goal for Nicole and I was to keep us below a ten minute pace for the entire race. It was way slower than I was accustomed to running, but then again I wasn't accustomed to running a marathon. I knew I had to be smart about pacing myself or I would never make it. I had to force myself to run at that pace so that I could survive the latter part of the race. We hit our first mile in about 10:20 due to all of the crowding on the bridge. I shouted out the time to Nicole and told her we were doing fine, that the slow time was because of the crowd. I felt great, and I could see the strength in Nicole's face, and in her stride next to me. I knew it was going to be a great race, and a great day! There were no spectators allowed on the bridge, but as we came off it into Brooklyn, thousands of people welcomed us cheering, holding up signs, and shouting out encouragement. It sent spine tingling adrenaline through my body. I really had to curb my enthusiasm and remember to focus on maintaining our pace and not running ahead. I felt like I could easily pop out some sub-seven minute miles. I knew what the consequences would be though, so I stuck to the plan. Nicole and I knew we could get through eighteen miles, but because our training suffered in the final weeks leading up to the marathon; we didn't know what to expect after that.

There were so many people lining the streets in Brooklyn that in most places they were eight to ten deep. There were bands on every ten or twenty blocks jamming out, and it was absolutely incredible. Nicole and I smiled at each other as we never expected the race to be so entertaining and exciting. We ran with gloves and hats on, and planned to toss them along the way when it warmed up. We ran next to each other zigzagging in and out of slower runners to keep our pace. There was so much commotion from the crowds and spectators that the miles just flew by. Before we knew it we were coming up on mile five. That's when Nicole started complaining about having to go to the bathroom.

"You're joking," I said.

"No Ben, I have to go."

"You're joking right?"

"No Ben I'm not, I have to go pee."

"Oh great Nicole, you have to be kidding me! We just came from the starting line where they had three-hundred shit pots lined up all the way up to the starting line and now you're telling me you have to go to the bathroom? You have to be fucking kidding me!"

"Just forget it," she said. "Just forget it!"

"I was so irritated. I shook my head as we ran wondering how she could have to go to the bathroom twenty minutes after we left the starting line." We argued for about another half mile.

"You have to be fucking kidding Nicole. If we stop we're going to add seven or eight minutes to our time! That's a lot. It would be the equivalent of a mile or more. You're going to screw up our time." I knew I was starting to be cruel, but I was angry that she hadn't used the bathroom at the starting line like I did. I even asked her, and she said she didn't have to go.

"Okay," I said as we ran together in the crowd, "Here's what we're going to do. I'm going to pick out a spot to go outside and we're going to make a pit stop as quick as possible and just go and get back into the race."

"I'm not doing that," she said.

"Nicole, you've done it before. Don't act like it's our first date. What about that time when we were camping?" She turned to me.

"Does this look like the Adirondacks, idiot?"

"Well that's our only option unless you want to be running through fucking Bed-Stuy by yourself!" She laughed at me, and then we both started laughing.

"Come on I said," and I bolted for a discreet area between two cars. She followed me and halfway there she turned back and started running back to the race.

"No way, I'm not going there! You're crazy." I started laughing.

"Okay, I'll find a better spot, but seriously this time we're stopping. I'll go too so there's no issue for the rest of the race." She looked over at me with a look of half acknowledgement, half wanting to kill me.

"Okay! Here we go, come on!," I said, and I bolted toward two humongous trucks parked next to each other in a Dunkin Donuts parking lot. Nicole followed, and within thirty seconds we had made the pit stop and came running back out from between the trucks and back into the race. We didn't miss a beat. I was laughing out loud the whole way. When we got back onto the race course beside each other I was still laughing and I looked over at Nicole. "Good job! You feel better?"

She didn't answer verbally, but gave me a quasi smile; a combination of "yes thank you that was a great idea we didn't ruin our time," and "you're an asshole!" I thought a quick argument and makeup was par for the course, just not after only five miles!

I was doing a great job of keeping us at a very comfortable 9:30 pace. I kept us on pace like clockwork, and I would know if we were off well before we came to a mile marker just by how my body felt. I was able to make adjustments and sometimes told Nicole we had to pick it up a little because we were falling off pace. I ran confidently and strong like my old self, and she knew I meant business. We passed mile marker seven and had become experts in grabbing a water or Gatorade off the table while running. It was a spectacle to see a couple hundred Dixie cups lined up on a table and dozens of runners passing by trying to grab a cup and keep their pace. Some runners stopped to drink, but we were all business and didn't stop for anything. We clumsily chugged down drinks while running, tossed the cups, and went right back to our mission. Just after mile seven we ran through Park Slope and Prospect Heights in Brooklyn. We were so stimulated by the crowds and bands lining each side of the street that we didn't even feel exerted. We felt as if we were on a tour of the five NYC Boroughs.

"Look how gorgeous those brownstones are." I pointed to them.

"Yeah, they're nice," she said. She seemed a little less distracted than I and more anxious about the race. As we ran through the two quaint neighborhoods, I was reminded again why I love the city so much. The neighborhood shops, brownstones, and old world charm were great. We had our names printed on our running jerseys like many of the other runners, and strangers in the crowd shouted at us throughout the run. People were great, and had no problem putting their own twists on our names as they cheered us on.

"Go Benny!"

"Go Nikki"

"Go Big Ben!"

"Go Ben and Nikki!"

At the halfway point of the race Nicole and I felt great. We felt as if we had only run a few miles. We alternated Gatorade and water along the route as necessary, and ate a couple gel packs to keep sugar in our blood. Brooklyn had a lot of alternative bands, rock bands, and a couple of Rap and R&B artists. As we entered Queens, there was a little more diversity in music. There was Freestyle, Spanish music, Rap, R&B, and Pop singers. It had a little more urban feel to it and people were still eight deep in many areas on the sides of the street. At around mile fourteen people were giving out bananas.

"Holy shit, look Nicole!" I laughed. "They're giving out bananas!" I took one as I ran by and bit into it obnoxiously. I turned with a big smile and looked back at Nicole holding it up and chewing. "You want a piece?" I asked with my mouth full.

"Oh my God. No Ben," she smiled shaking her head.

"It's so good. You think they'll have burgers next?" I yelled out. All the runners around us burst out laughing, and I smiled and finished the banana.

A few minutes later we came to the 59th Street Bridge. I looked over at Nicole running strong beside me. "Okay, let's rock!" I said. "The bridge is going to be steep so let's make sure we keep the pace."

"Okay," she said. We had heard this was one of the toughest parts of the race because three quarters of the bridge was on an incline. There is an upper and lower level of the bridge, but we were stuck running on the lower level. We chopped away at it and eventually it flattened out and we were able to catch our breath.

"Stay with me," I said to Nicole, and I moved to the center of the bridge. "I read an article that people stop and piss off the upper level and the wind blows it back on the people running on the lower level below."

"Are you serious?" she laughed.

"Yeah, Sal told me one of his friends ran last year and people were screaming because they were getting sprayed in the face! Imagine?"

"No, that's disgusting."

"Yup," I said. People were stopping on the sides of the bridge to take pictures every few hundred feet. *Silly,* I thought. I wasn't stopping for anything until I crossed the finish line.

As we started coming down the other side of the bridge I heard what sounded like muffled thunder. As we got closer I realized it wasn't thunder, but was the roar of the crowd in Manhattan welcoming runners. The closer we got the louder it got. As we came off the bridge into Manhattan people were twenty to thirty deep on both sides of the road cheering. The sound was deafening. I had never seen anything like it, nor did I expect it. People hung out the windows of their buildings, held up signs, and screamed and hollered at us. *Eye of the Tiger* played on huge speakers, and all I could think about was how unreal the whole experience was. If ever an opportunity allowed me to stop time, this would be it. I was so pumped, and it dawned on me that there was no way in hell I was going to fail. I ran with strength and spring in my legs as if we just started the race, and Nicole did the same. We headed up First Avenue looking forward to passing our parents and friends cheering at 73rd Street.

"They said stay to the left," said Nicole.

"Okay," I said.

First Avenue was great. The sidewalks were so full on each side of the street that it looked like the spectators couldn't move. We ran on the left side of the street close to the curb, hoping to see our families. As we got a block away from 73rd street we could see the big neon green signs my stepdad Ed had made, waving in the air. We got closer and as we ran by, all of our family and friends were hanging over the fence cheering for us. Our three parents were in the front, and when my mother saw us she screamed at the top of her lungs. Nicole's mom was right up front and it made her race! Ali stretched out her arm, and Nicole ran up close to get the power bars from her. I flashed a peace sign as we continued on, and within seconds we were further up the block away from them, and coming up on mile seventeen. I never understood why people ran marathons, but by the time we were at mile seventeen I knew exactly why. It's an extraordinary experience that you can only comprehend by actually participating in one.

The crowds continued all the way up First Avenue until we got close to the Bronx where it thinned out a bit. Bands continued to appear every now and then jamming out and rejuvenating our spirits, but for the first time I started feeling beat up. My heart, felt fantastic which I was thrilled about, but my legs started cramping so badly that I wasn't sure I was going to make it.

"Ouch! My legs are cramping really bad Nicole!"

"You can do it," she said.

"No you don't understand it's not about will power. I'm not going to be able to continue physically if my legs keep cramping like this. They're starting to feel like I can't move them."

"You'll be okay. Let's go!" she said. I continued jogging and wincing. I knew we were off pace, and I was getting pissed.

"We're off pace," I said.

"Ben, we're just looking to finish. That's enough about the pace!" My quadriceps were contracting when my feet hit the ground like they were supposed to, but the problem was that they weren't loosening up between strides! They would contract and stay contracted, and it was so painful. I drank Gatorade at the water station hoping that electrolytes would alleviate the cramping, and I took a gel pack.

We crossed into the Bronx at around mile twenty, and I was in complete agony. I looked down at my watch and our split for that mile was 11:40. I was getting very nervous. My mind was in the race and I felt great cardiovascularly, but I was concerned that my legs were going to be my demise. They felt like two pieces of steel with no spring in them and electricity shocking them to stay contracted. As we came off the bridge a miracle happened. I heard a beat that I recognized faintly in the distance. As we got closer Nicole and I looked at each other and smiled.

"You hear that?" I yelled. "That's *Wifey*, by *Next*!"

"I know," she said.

"Let's go!" I said picking the pace back up. It got us amped up and distracted enough to keep pushing. *Wifey* and *Next* were sentimental favorites from when I was courting Nicole as a bachelor. It was the epitome of a great R&B song and brought back memories of us dating, and going clubbing in Manhattan. Coincidentally it was our saving grace in the Bronx. We weren't in the Bronx for more than a mile or so, and then we headed back into Manhattan for the final few miles of the race. The bands and crowds picked up again as we came down 5th Avenue into Harlem. People had been dropping like flies from the Bronx right on down. Nicole was looking tired, but not hurting as badly as I with my leg cramping. We hit a water stop and she was in front of me when I stumbled. I didn't have the strength in my legs to keep from smashing on the ground and I reached out and leaned on her shoulder to avoid falling to the pavement. As I did my legs locked up, and she was so weak herself that I nearly brought us both down.

"What are you doing!" she screamed at me. I regained my balance and started laughing. It was that *charlie horse* pain kind of laugh, not because anything was funny. Nicole looked at me angrily.

"What the hell's the matter with you?" she asked.

"I'm sorry, I didn't mean it. My legs are shot. Are you okay? If I didn't lean on you I would have fallen. I'm really sorry I didn't mean it. I hope I can make it to the finish." I started getting a little flustered. I was pushing myself as hard as I could and getting nervous for the first time about my heart. I wondered if it was going to hold up. It felt okay, but I was really straining now and had anxiety about a stitch coming loose, beat irregularities, or general inability of the repaired heart to keep up with the severe demand I was putting on it. *Wouldn't it be silly if I dropped dead now,* I thought. Instinctually I kept pushing, with no regard for the potential consequences.

"Come on it's not much further," Nicole said. Coming down 5th Avenue was tough. Everyone around us was slowing up, and some people were mixing in walking with running.

"There's no way in hell we're walking any part of this race," I said to Nicole. "I just hope my legs last long enough to get me to the finish."

"Come on," she said. "Just keep going, we're almost there."

"Who are you kidding Nicole?" I laughed. "Besides the mileage, you have no idea where the hell we are." We both laughed. Mile twenty-four to twenty-five was another tough one. I had intended to be running eight something per mile for the last few miles, but my body had an entirely different plan. I pushed as hard as I could yet the last few miles were between ten and eleven minutes. I was so annoyed. We ran as hard as we could for the last 1.2 miles of the race.

"We have to break 4:30, we have to!" I said as we pushed each other.

"Yeah, we won't make the NY Times if we come in over 4:30!" Nicole reminded me.

The crowds roared. People screamed, and air horns and noisemakers went off. Huge flat screen monitors showed us as we passed by, and news trucks and video cameras were everywhere. We entered Central Park at mile twenty-six.

As we came up Park Drive Nicole shouted "Get over to the right near the grandstands, we need to wave to your parents." At that point my legs were so heavy I felt like there were cinderblocks strapped to my feet. "Come on! Come on!" shouted Nicole, pushing the pace.

I reached out my hand and she grabbed it. A moment later we saw my parents coming up on the right side leaning over the fence of the VIP grandstands. Everything cut to slow motion. They were both holding huge "Go Team Carey" signs and shouting at the top of their lungs. My mom had tears in her eyes and they both cheered us on as we ran by. Nicole and I waved and hollered to them. I flashed my two finger salute, and we were in the home stretch. We squeezed each other's hands and ran as fast as we could. A moment later we crossed the finish line throwing up our arms shouting. I looked down at my watch. We had finished in four hours and twenty-three minutes.

"Yes! We did it!" I shouted. Nicole was bent over with her head between her legs. I put my hand on her back. "Come on babe, you need to keep moving or you'll get sick."

"Abababababa" she babbled. She was exhausted. She grabbed my hand and we walked through the finishers chute. A woman put medals around our necks and took our picture. The medals were large medallions, and heavier than I expected.

"Ahhhhh," I said to Nicole as we kept walking. "We did it. We fucking did it! I can't believe it. You know; it really wasn't that bad. Everyone should do the NYC Marathon once in their life. I can't believe what an experience that was. You would never guess it to be like that."

We continued walking through the chute, and they gave us foil wraps to put around ourselves to stay warm. They also gave us some snacks to get our blood sugar back up. The finishing chute was the most annoying part of the day, as it took us about forty minutes to get out of it. Apparently they made it that way to avoid having finishers spill into the streets immediately outside of the finish line causing a ruckus. We must have walked a good mile or two confined to the chute. Toward the end Nicole didn't look well. She was shivering uncontrollably, so I gave her my thermal wrap and hugged her to try and warm her up. Finally we got out of the park at about 86th Street and Central Park West.

"I have to use the bathroom really bad," said Nicole. "I think I'm going to be sick."

"Okay, well go ahead, there's a porta-potty right there."

She went in and was there for a good ten minutes and then in typical Nicole fashion I hear a loud, "Benjamin!?" A dozen people sitting on benches along the park looked over at the porta-potty, and then turned to me.

"Yes?" I said (now on stage).

"I need toilet paper!"

I laughed out loud. "Uhm, okay. Well that's gonna be a problem because there is none."

"Benjamin!" she yelled.

The people on the benches and some other bystanders were all smirking and watching this sitcom go down. It was like an episode from *Curb your Enthusiasm*. A nice old man, feeling my pain offered some advice.

"Check over there, I bet they have something to help you," he smiled. He motioned to a nearby medical tent. I pointed my index finger at him like *Bill Parcells* telling a player good job, and then walked over to the tent. The nurses there were helping a couple of sick runners, so I helped myself to the paper towel roll on the table and made a bee line for the porta-potty. I knocked on the door and handed them inside to Nicole. A few minutes later she came out, and the door slammed shut behind her. The people on the bench looked over, and I gave the old man on the bench a wink and a thumbs-up. Nicole caught it and her eyes widened looking me straight in the eye. We both started laughing and then started walking down Central Park West to meet my parents at 67th Street, our agreed upon meeting place. We were spent, but walking on air after completing the marathon.

My parents spotted us walking in the crowd along Central Park West almost an hour after we first crossed the finish line. I saw my mom approaching, holding the huge green sign over her head yelling "Go Team Carey!" My stepdad Ed was trailing right behind her filming our reunion on video. My mom is a small woman with wavy brown hair and brown eyes. People always comment on how beautiful she is. Nicole and I laughed hysterically when we saw her approaching with the huge sign over her head, struggling to hold it up.

"Congratulations!" Ed said as he gave me a big hug. Nicole and my mom exchanged hugs. "That's my girl," she said, and then she gave me a big hug too.

"Amazing, Ben," she said. "That was an experience of a lifetime. When you guys ran by at 73rd Street it took my breath away. Watching you cross the finish line with Nicole holding your hand brought me to tears. The last time I felt so exhilarated was the day I gave birth to you. I didn't think you could ever make me feel that way again. When you crossed the finish line I was left breathless, laughing, and crying at the same time."

"Thanks a lot Mom. I'm glad you guys were here. Did you guys see Dr. Stewart finish?"

"No," said Ed. "He should have just finished because I was tracking him on my Ipad. Sal finished a few minutes before you guys. You were pretty close."

There were still many streets closed off, and crowds of people roaming all over so we decided to walk through the park to the east side where the bar we were meeting at was located. My parents seemed just as elated as us about the whole day. Nicole's mom was waiting at the bar for us with the rest of our family and friends. The walk to the finish line from the bar was too much for her so she waited there for us. Nicole called her on the walk over.

"Mom, why are you crying?.......oh, thanks! You don't have to cry Mom.......yeah I'm okay." Emotions were running high. "Okay Mom, we'll see you in a few minutes we're almost there."

"Is everything okay?" I asked Nicole.

"Yeah, my Mom is just happy. I didn't think she would enjoy this so much. She's overwhelmed." I was glad that Nicole's mom came in with my parents to watch the race and support us. It meant a lot to me, but I knew it meant even more to Nicole. I thought about Dr. Stewart and borrowed my mom's cell phone to shoot him a quick text message to see how he did, and let him know where we were headed. The walk through the park took about fifteen minutes, and we hailed a cab on the other side to bring us to the bar. I hadn't realized how sore my legs were until I tried to sit down in the cab. My legs were too weak to support my weight, and I dropped heavily like a rock into the seat.

When we got out of the taxi at the bar, strangers in the street were walking up to us congratulating us because they saw the medals hanging around our necks. I grunted loudly and could barely lift my legs to make it up the step to get inside. Sal and Ali's families were there, and everyone exchanged hugs. The Rayfields and Merlinos congratulated us, and it felt good to be done. Nicole's mom came up with tears in her eyes and gave us both big hugs. We also finally got to see Sal for the first time since we left the starting line together earlier that morning.

"How'd it go?" he asked as he hugged Nicole.

"Awesome!" said Nicole. "It was an experience I'll never forget."

"Yeah, I didn't expect it to be like that," I chimed in. "It was incredible. Dr. Singer told me the run over the Verrazano Bridge and through Brooklyn was going to be amazing, and to make sure I took it all in, but I didn't expect it to be like that. We really had a lot of fun."

"How do you feel?" I asked Sal.

"Look," he said. He took off his sneaker to reveal a blood soaked sock. "You don't want to see the rest. I got a really bad blister halfway through the race. It was really painful to run on."

"Oh, that sucks man. I'm really sorry Sal. I know you would have run a hell of a lot faster, but you still ran a great time."

"It was awesome to see all of the people and bands and excitement. I enjoyed it," he said.

We hung out for about a half hour, during which time I got a congratulatory text message back from Dr. Stewart. He was also exhausted, so we made plans to have dinner another time to celebrate. On the drive back to Long Island our parents talked more about the day than we did. They went on and on about how many people were there, people they met, and how exciting the day was. Nicole and I were very mellow and relaxed. When we got home we saw cute signs taped to the front door saying *Good Job Mommy and Daddy* with all sorts of artwork. The kids had just finished baking a cake with their *Aunt Shelly,* Nicole's twin sister, and they ran to greet us.

"Mommy we saw you on TV," said Preston.

"Yeah, and so did the neighbors," said Milan. We laughed, and then we all sat down to eat the burgers we had stopped for on the way home. Nicole savored her burger and a frosted mug of Guinness, and I was so tired I could barely stay awake to finish eating. Our parents were still going on about the day, and our kids were asking dozens of questions.

When everyone had left and the kids had gone to bed, Nicole and I sat together in the red chair near the fireplace in the great room. I gazed through tired eyes at the flickering flames, and then I looked up at the thirty foot wall of glass with French doors; framed by two tremendous curtains pulled back on each side. My eyes welled up and I got a lump in my throat. In my mind I followed the intricate woodwork and traced the lines of all the French panes, and I thought of Brian McAvey. He will always be a part of me and my home.

The warmth from the fireplace felt great on our sore muscles, and we dozed off in each other's arms. I dreamt that night a familiar dream; one I thought I had lost after my heart surgery because it ceased to visit me any longer. It is a dream that started when I met Nicole and more valuable to me than material wealth, or anything earthly.

I dreamt of growing old and gray with my wife; my kindred spirit. An orange sun setting low in the sky cast a sepia glow on this existence. It appears as a grainy, choppy, old fashioned film. Our energies are softened with age, and lines in our skin are evidence of days gone by. Our home with big white pillars is stately but withering, and the overgrown landscaping complements it like a bottle of fine Barolo. We sit in our wooden rockers on the front porch in this dream; sipping iced tea, and watching our grandchildren run and play in the tall grass, catching fireflies at dusk. The huge rock in the background casts a long shadow. Today I live another day.

Are you a Heartosaurus?

www.heartosaurus.com